PAPER
CREATIONS

PAPER CREATIONS

◆

Easy-to-Make Paperfolding Projects

Gay Merrill Gross

Principal Photographers
Ellen Silverman and Nancy Palubniak

FRIEDMAN/FAIRFAX
PUBLISHERS

A FRIEDMAN/FAIRFAX BOOK

© 1997 by Michael Friedman Publishing Group, Inc.

Library of Congress Cataloging-in Publication Data

Gross, Gay Merrill.
    Paper creations : easy-to-make paperfolding projects / Gay Merrill
Gross ; principal photographers, Ellen Silverman and Nancy
Palubniak.
    p. cm.
        Includes index
        ISBN 1-56799-439-3
        1. Paper work. 2. Origami. I. Title.
TT870.G795   1997   96-51838
736' .982--dc21   CIP

Editors: Sharyn Rosart, Nathaniel Marunas, Tony Burgess
Designer: Jennifer Blanc
Illustrators: Steve Arcella and Katherine Fuetsch
Original Diagrams: Gay Merrill Gross
Photography Director: Christopher C. Bain
Project Photography © Ellen Silverman and © Nancy Palubniak
Production Manager: Jeanne Hutter

Color separations by Bright Arts Graphics (S) Pte Ltd Co.
Printed in China by Leefung-Asco Printers Ltd.

10 9 8 7 6 5 4 3 2 1

For bulk purchases and specials sales, please contact:
Friedman/Faifax Publishers
Attention: Sales Department
15 West 26th Street
New York, New York 10010
212/685-6610 FAX 212/685-1307

Materials in this volume have been previously published in
Origami: Creative Ideas for Paperfolding (Friedman/Fairfax, 1990)
and *The Origami Workshop* (Friedman/Fairfax, 1995).

Visit our website:
http://www.metrobooks.com

ACKNOWLEDGMENTS

This book represents a collection not only of original origami models but also of creative ideas, all generously shared. When Lillian Oppenheimer founded The Origami Center of America, her desire to share and spread origami set the tone and spirit that has promoted such a free exchange among paperfolders.

Thank you to all who have contributed designs, creative ideas, and other assistance in the production of this book.

In particular, I would like to thank:

The creators of the models diagrammed in this book; Paolo Bascetta, Ranana Benjamin, Sam Ciulla, Rae Cooker, Gloria Farison, Alice Gray, Thomas Hull, Humiaki Huzita, Rachel Katz, Yoshihide Momotani, Ralph Matthews, Robert Neale, Lillian Oppenheimer (on behalf of Molly Kahn), Aldo Putignano, Nick Robinson, Lewis Simon, Mitsunobu Sonobe, E.D. Sullivan, Florence Temko, and Mike Thomas.

For sharing their ideas and expertise in special techniques, Don Sigal (Photocopier Designs); deg farrelly (Paper Bonding); Mark Kennedy and Becky Berman (Protective Coatings); Ros Joyce and Mark Kennedy (Wet Folding); Alice Gray and Michael Shall (Gluing Tips); Alice Gray, Mark Kennedy, and Jean Baden-Gillette (Origami Jewelry); and Kathleen O'Regan (Map Folding).

For ideas for arrangement of flower models, Idan Schwartz (Tulip) and Sara Goldhaber (Buttonhole Flower).

For sample models used in photographs, Aldo Putignano (Bowls) and John Blackman (Necklace).

For research material, Mark Kennedy, Michael Shall, David Lister, and Laura Kruskal.

A special thank you to Pearl Chin for all her generous help, and to John Blackman, who designed many of the useful items for the Crane, Hexahedron, and Fluted Diamond models, and loaned us some of his creations for photographing.

Paper sources: Kotobuki Trading Company, San Francisco, California; Sopp America, Inc., Dayton, New Jersey; and A Thousand Cranes, New York, New York.

Thank you to my mother, who not only handed me my first origami book when I was nine years old, but has encouraged my fascination with folded paper ever since.

My own knowledge and education in the folding arts are enhanced by my many wonderful associations and friendships made through The Friends of the Origami Center of America, now renamed Origami USA. Thank you to Michael Shall, who founded this forum for folders, and to Lillian Oppenheimer, whose generous and sharing nature has laid the foundation for many organizations around the world devoted to paperfolding.

Table of Contents

Introduction
A History of Paperfolding

A folk art, a creative art, a mathematical puzzle, a game—all of these terms can be used to describe origami. Some people are attracted to origami for its simplicity, while others marvel at the minds of the people who are able to devise the patterns for some of the ingenious creations. Some look to origami as a way of entertaining, while others find it has a calming, relaxing effect.

Origami is unique among papercrafts in that it requires no materials other than the paper itself. Cutting, gluing, or drawing on the paper is avoided, in favor of folding to create the desired results. No special skills or artistic talent are needed for origami, although a good amount of patience and perseverance are very helpful. Models can be made by following instructions exactly or by varying the folds to create something a little different. Experimenting with the paper may also lead you to design a totally new, original paperfold.

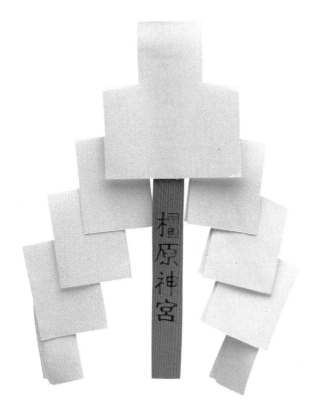

The importance of the *go-hei* in the Shinto religion illustrates the reverence the Japanese give to the qualities of pure white paper.

The word *origami* comes from the Japanese language. *Ori* means folded and *kami* means paper. When the two words are combined, the *k* from kami becomes a *g*, giving us *origami*. Paperfolding as a traditional folk art pervaded the Japanese culture more strongly than any other. But traditional paperfolding did not exist in Japan alone, so we will try to go back and trace the roots of paperfolding around the world.

Reconstructing a history of paperfolding is more a matter of conjecture and supposition than of hard facts. It is probable that the art began in China, where papermaking methods were first developed two thousand years ago. Although certain traditional designs such as the junk and pagoda are generally attributed to the Chinese, no records accounting for the time or place of their creation can confirm this or tell us just how old these folds are. Evidence of paperfolding in China is often associated with the Chinese tradition of re-creating small objects used during a person's life and then burying or burning them with a deceased person. This practice of funerary folds is still carried out today in areas strongly influenced by Chinese religion and culture, such as Hong Kong and Singapore.

Papermaking techniques were not readily shared by the Chinese but did eventually travel to Korea and then Japan by the seventh century. The closely guarded knowledge then spread in the direction of the Arab world, reaching Spain by the twelfth century. During this journey, did simple paperfolding principles spread with the knowledge of making the paper? Or did each country independently discover that paper could not only be written and drawn on, but manipulated into forms by creating a pattern of creases? Despite the similarity of some traditional models associated with different paperfolding traditions (the Japanese boat with sail and the Spanish *pajarita*, for example), most people believe that there was little commingling of paperfolding ideas until the end of the nineteenth century.

THE JAPANESE TRADITION

The Japanese have always had a reverence for the special qualities of paper. Even the Japanese word for paper, *kami*, is pronounced identically (although the characters are written differently) as their word for God. For more than a thousand years, paper has played a prominent part in the Shinto religion. Streamers of white paper cut into a zigzag pattern are called *o-shide*, or *go-hei* when found in pairs. O-shide are placed at the entrances to Shinto shrines while go-hei are found in a place of honor inside the shrine, denoting the presence of the deity.

The first Japanese paperfolds did not seek to create the likeness of any living or material object but were merely abstract, decorative forms used for ceremonial purposes. These early paperfolds, believed to date back to the twelfth century, are folded ornaments called *noshi*. A noshi is attached to a package to signify that it is a gift (serving the same purpose as a bow in Western culture). It also symbolizes a wish for the recipient's good fortune. The standardized manner for folding noshi involved pleating the paper at prescribed, irregular angles, not an easy task. Etiquette required that young women be skilled in folding noshi. It has been theorized that simple, representational paperfolds that would appeal to children evolved as a way of exercising young fingers. This would give them practice in working with the intricate and difficult patterns of the noshi. The custom of attaching a noshi to a gift still continues today, but it is rare to find someone folding their own noshi. Commercially made noshi are now available in Japanese stores.

In 1845, a volume in a Japanese collection called the *Kan-no-mado* showed drawings and some sketchy diagrams for making more than forty folded figures. This publication, one of the earliest to record the folding pattern for an origami model, shows that origami had reached a stage of greater intricacy and broader scope than the folding of the decorative noshi or simple toylike figures. It also shows us that the rules of traditional Japanese origami did not prohibit the use of slits in or drawings on the paper.

THE WESTERN TRADITION

The most well-known and possibly the oldest paperfold in Europe is an abstract design of a small bird (*pajarita*) that originated in Spain but was known throughout Europe. In France the design was a hen, in Germany a crow, and in England a hobbyhorse.

Evidence of the popularity of the pajarita can be found in its occasional appearance in late-nineteenth-century drawings and paintings. But this traditional paperfold was probably known much earlier than that. The same creases used for folding the pajarita are found in folded baptismal certificates that date back to eighteenth-century Germany. By the mid-nineteenth century, there were quite a few decorative and playful paperfolds known in Europe, many of them based on the same folding pattern as the pajarita. During this period, German educator Friedrich Froebel, who founded the kindergarten based on his philosophy that children learn from play, promoted paperfolding as a learning exercise for children.

Several traditional Western folds were neither handed down from mother to child as in Japan nor taught in a formal educational setting. These "playground folds" were taught by one child to another. The paper airplane, the newspaper hat, and the fortune-teller, or cootie catcher, are all examples of traditional Western paperfolds.

In both the East and the West, paperfolding experienced a transition from ceremonial to playful folds to use in education, and finally to its present status as a creative art and craft.

In Spain the *pajarita* (little bird) is as widely recognized as the paper airplane is in North America.

CREATIVE PAPERFOLDING

One of the first persons to experiment creatively with paperfolding was Spanish philosopher Miguel de Unamuno (1864–1936). Although some of his designs were published, they reached only a very limited audience. The main influence of Unamuno's work was in promoting the idea of creative folding among the folders of Spain. Several of these Spanish paperfolders eventually migrated to Argentina around the time of the Spanish civil war (1936) and continued this creative approach there.

Far more influential were the explorations of some of the Japanese folders of the early twentieth century. Most important among them was Akira Yoshizawa. Yoshizawa, who was born in 1911, has devoted a lifetime to origami. His designs, techniques, and use of paper all represent the work of an artist and creative genius. Fortunately, his work became well-known throughout the world. Through contacts with the West, he has had many exhibitions of his work in Europe and the United States, special classes have been organized, and most important, his designs have been made available to other folders all over the world thanks to the dozen or so books he has written.

Almost as important as Yoshizawa's advances in creative folding is the diagramming system he developed that uses easily understood symbols. This symbol notation was adopted with some modifications by authors Robert Harbin and Samuel Randlett and used in their classic books *The Art of Origami* (Randlett, 1961) and *Secrets of Origami* (Harbin, 1964). They have subsequently become the standard symbols for origami books written around the world. This internationally understood symbol notation makes it possible to follow the pictorial explanations for folding a model even if the text is written in a language you don't understand. Publishing a new origami design today means that it can be immediately shared with an international community. What a difference from the early years in our paper history, when it took more than a thousand years for papermaking techniques to spread from China to Europe.

Today, origami is an international creative pastime. Building upon the basics of the traditional Eastern and Western designs, many folders around the world have followed the creative path of leaders such as Yoshizawa and Unamuno and are devising their own new designs. The repertoire of a couple hundred traditional folds that existed at the beginning of the twentieth century has grown in the latter half of the twentieth century to tens of thousands of new designs, with an endless number yet to be discovered.

One of the reasons for origami's change from a relatively static, traditional folk art to an ever-changing creative art was the increased availability of paper. The first model for a papermaking machine was created in Europe in 1798. Up until that time, every sheet was created by hand, one at a time. With that in mind, it makes sense that paperfolding as a leisurely activity did not catch on in a big way until paper became less expensive and available in greater supply. Another reason was the ability to record folding instruction in books. This meant that paperfolding designs were no longer limited to a few simple figures a mother could memorize and then teach to a young child.

The first records of paperfolding were drawings of finished figures with no explanations of how to make them. Just as the pajarita appeared in drawings and paintings in Europe, so did the crane, or *tsuru*, in Japan. At least one or two Japanese books that show folding methods predate the *Kan-no-mado* of 1845. One of these was called *Sembazuru Orikata* (Folding a Thousand Cranes), which was published in 1797. This book showed how to fold families of multiple connected cranes from single sheets of paper cut into a series of connecting squares.

The occasional book on paperfolding started appearing in English in the first half of the twentieth century. These books, such as Murray and Rigney's *Paperfolding for Fun,* were all comprised of traditional models. The first book in English to suggest that origami could be a creative art was Robert Harbin's *Paper Magic,* first published in England in 1956. Harbin, a South African-born stage magician living in England, was fortunate to have contact with Ligia Montoya and the Japanese origami master Akira Yoshizawa. Montoya lived in Argentina and was a disciple of Unamuno's school of Spanish folding. Their influence on Harbin was reflected in the many books Harbin wrote on origami, which in turn influenced hundreds of paperfolders, many of whom eventually contacted the author. One such person was a fifty-eight-year-old woman in New York City who enjoyed making things with her hands, although she had never thought she was particularly good at it. The success she had with paperfolding delighted her so much that she could not understand why everyone in the world would not want to learn this remarkable activity. Lillian Oppenheimer began collecting every model and book on origami she could find

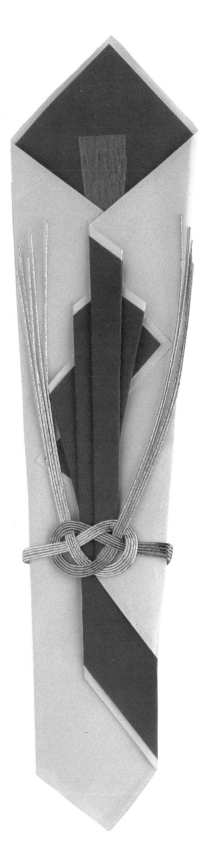

The noshi is an example of Japanese ceremonial paperfolding. (From the collection of Lore Schirokauer.)

at the time. The new models she learned she taught to others and encouraged them to teach as well. Her enthusiasm and desire to learn and share more led her in 1958 to found the Origami Center of America. Thanks to this forum for bringing folders together, the cross-fertilization of creative ideas increased the depth and appeal of this art. What was originally considered a children's activity was now attracting the interest of mathematicians, engineers, scientists, computer programmers, college professors, and professional artists.

The Origami Center offered classes and meetings for paperfolders. They held annual conventions, published a newsletter, and sold origami books and paper. In later years, paperfolders in many other countries followed Lillian Oppenheimer's example and started their own origami societies. In 1980, The Friends of The Origami Center of America was founded by paperfolder Michael Shall to continue Lillian Oppenheimer's origami activities. In 1994, the organization's name was changed to Origami USA.

Today, the organization has a membership of almost two thousand paperfolders around the world.

The models in this book reflect the international nature of origami today. Creators from the United States, England, France, Italy, Japan, and Argentina have all contributed designs. The models also represent origami's past and present. From the past are several classic designs that were favorites more than one hundred years ago and have lasted to become even more well known and appealing in present times. From the multitude of modern designs, those presented here offer examples of some of the popular themes in origami today, such as action toys, practical origami, and modulars (constructions of several interlocking units). But most important, the models in this book were chosen for their ability to delight and fascinate both the folders and those with whom they share their art. Hopefully, you also will be enchanted and inspired by these designs' charm and ingenuity.

Published in 1797, *Sembazuru Orikata* (Folding a Thousand Cranes), showed how to make families of cranes such as these. Slits are cut as shown. The circle indicates where the head is folded.

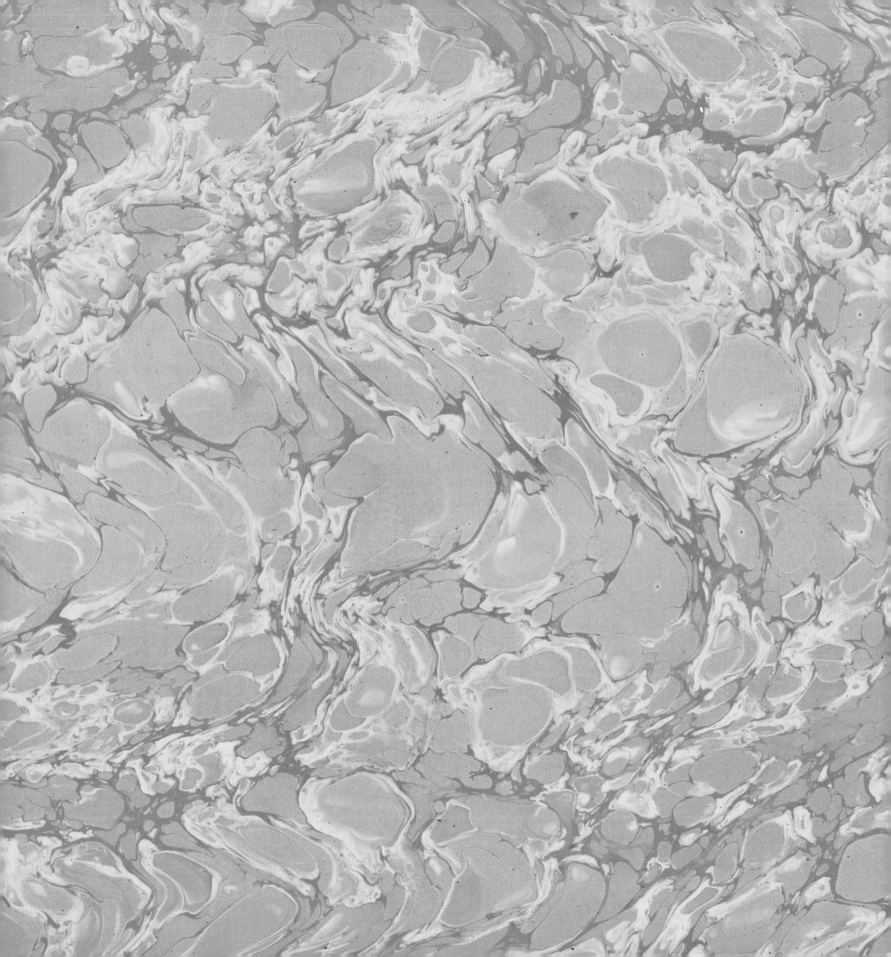

◆ *Part I*
INTRODUCTION TO ORIGAMI

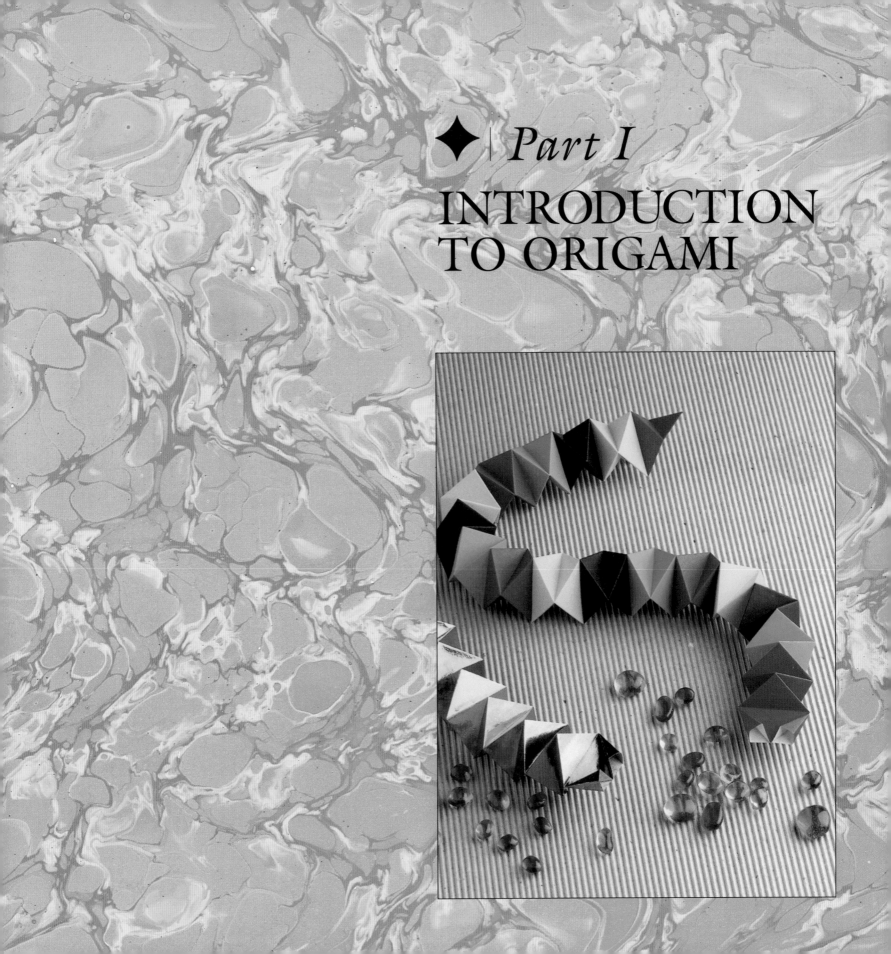

ORIGAMI SYMBOLS

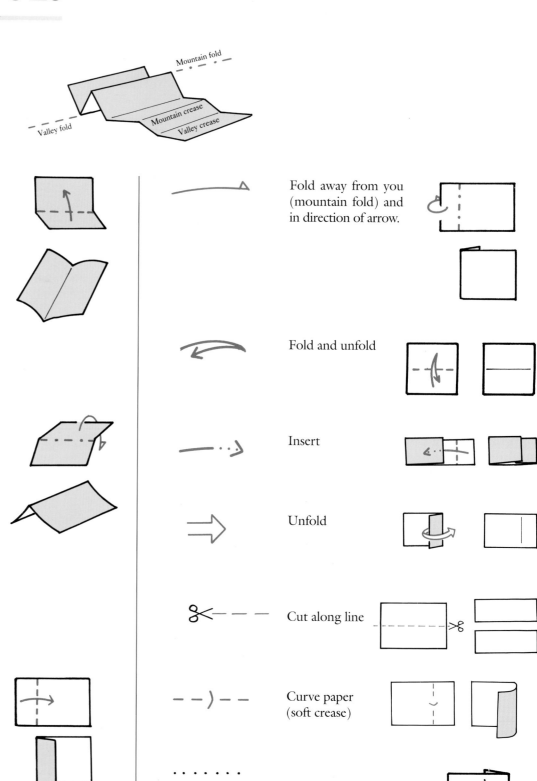

VALLEY FOLD:
Fold paper forward

When you open paper that has been valley-folded, you will see a concave crease that bends inward like a groove, or valley. This is called a valley crease.

MOUNTAIN FOLD:
Fold paper backward

When you open paper that has been mountain–folded, you will see a convex crease that bends outward—it has a little peak you can pinch. This is called a mountain crease.

Fold toward you (valley fold) and in direction of arrow.

Fold away from you (mountain fold) and in direction of arrow.

Fold and unfold

Insert

Unfold

Cut along line

Curve paper (soft crease)

X-ray view

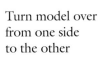	Turn model over from one side to the other	
	Scale of drawing enlarges	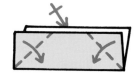
	Repeat here	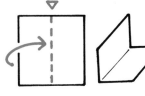
6-8	Repeat step 6 through 8 here	
90° 	Form a right angle	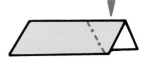
	Push here	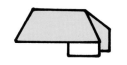
	Hold here	

	Rotate paper one half turn (top of model will rotate to bottom)	
	Rotate paper one quarter turn (top of model will rotate to side)	
	Rotate paper one eighth turn (top of model will rotate to side)	
	Match the dots	

Raw Edge

Crease

Folded Edge

Double Raw Edge

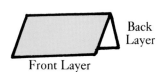

Front Layer

Back Layer

15

BASIC FOLDS

Folding patterns that are commonly used throughout origami are given easy-to-remember names based on what they look like when the folds are completed.

BOOK FOLD

Fold one side edge over to lie on opposite side edge.

DIAPER FOLD

Fold one corner to lie over opposite corner.

CUPBOARD FOLD

Fold two opposite parallel sides towards each other to meet at center.

ICE CREAM CONE FOLD

Fold two adjacent sides to meet at center.

 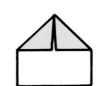

HOUSE ROOF FOLD

Fold two adjacent corners to meet at center.

BLINTZ FOLD

Fold all four corners to meet at center.

Note: Although less easily recognizable, the crease pattern for a sideways ice cream cone fold is still called an "ice cream cone fold." The same is true for all the basic folds.

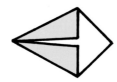

Still an ice cream cone fold.

Still a book fold.

Still a cupboard fold.

REVERSE FOLDS

INSIDE REVERSE FOLD

In order for you to perform a reverse fold, your model or portion of model should have a front layer, a back layer, and a folded edge or spine connecting the two layers. In a reverse fold, an end of this double layer of paper is turned either into itself (inside reverse fold) or around itself (outside reverse fold).

1 You may wish to prepare your paper first by performing a simple valley fold that will serve as a precrease.

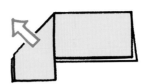

2 Check to be sure this is the shape you would like the paper to ultimately take, then unfold.

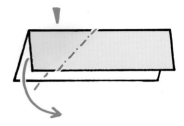

3 Spread the layers of your paper apart. Apply pressure (push in) at the mountain folded edge (spine) until it changes to a valley fold. At the same time, the precreases you made earlier will both become mountain folded edges.

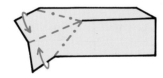

4 This shows the inside reverse fold in progress. Keep applying pressure to end of paper until model can be flattened.

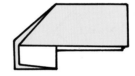

5 One end of your double layer is now "sandwiched" between the front and back layers.

OUTSIDE REVERSE FOLD

Again, starting with front and back layers connected by a "spine," you can "wrap" one end around both layers, as if turning a hood onto your head.

1 Mark the place where you want the fold to be (precrease). Unfold.

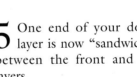

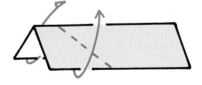

2 Spread the layers apart and wrap end around outside of model.

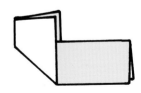

3 Press flat.

FOLDING HINTS

- It is usually easier to fold paper on a hard surface such as a table.

- Fold as neatly and as accurately as you can.

- If the paper you are using is colored or patterned on one side only: origami directions usually specify which side should be facing up when you begin folding. If this is not indicated, it is usually safe to begin with the white side of the paper facing you.

- It is usually easier to fold paper by bringing an edge from the lower part of the paper up. If you find it easier to fold this way and directions indicate a side-to-side or downward fold, you can always rotate your paper so that the direction of the fold is now upward, and then fold. After folding, reposition your paper so that it looks like the next step in the diagram.

- It is usually easier to make a valley fold in your model than to make a mountain fold. A valley fold becomes a mountain fold when you turn your paper over, so if a diagram indicates to make a mountain fold, you may choose to turn the paper over and make a valley fold. When you turn your paper back to the right side, you will see the desired mountain fold.

- Origami diagrams are usually drawn as if the paper were held loosely rather than pressed flat. This slightly three-dimensional representation is used to give you information about the different layers of paper. If you see a slight gap between edges in a diagram, this would disappear if model were pressed flat.

- In general, your paper should be folded right to an edge or crease, *without* leaving a gap, unless otherwise indicated in the written instructions.

ORIGAMI BASES

DIAMOND BASE

Begin with white side up.

> A combination of folding patterns that gives you a specific form is called an origami base. Most origami models use one of these bases as a starting point.

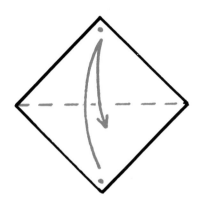

1 Lay square on table so one corner is near you. Bring that corner up to top corner. Crease and unfold.

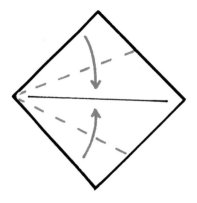

2 Ice cream cone fold: Bring two raw edges that join at left-side corner together to lie on horizontal center line.

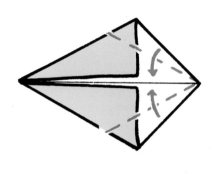

3 Bring raw edges that join at right corner to horizontal center line.

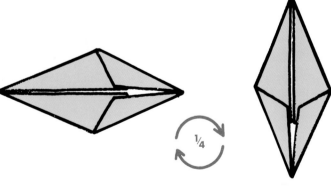

4 Rotate model so that right corner is now at bottom of model.

5 Completed diamond base.

PRELIMINARY BASE

Begin with a square, white side facing up.

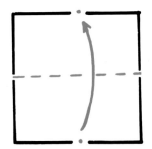 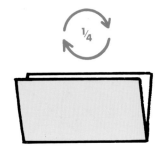 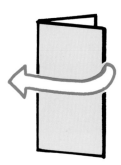 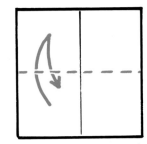

1 Bring bottom raw edge up to meet top raw edge. When edges and corners meet exactly, run your hand along folded edge to form a sharp crease. The fold you have just made is called a book fold.

2 Rotate your paper so the folded edge is now vertical.

3 Unfold—open the book.

4 Book fold and unfold: You should have a crease marking the vertical center line of your square. Bring the raw edge now at the bottom of your square up to meet the top raw edge. Crease and unfold.

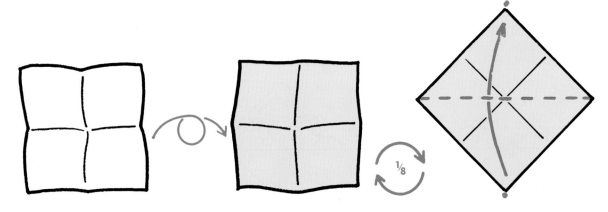 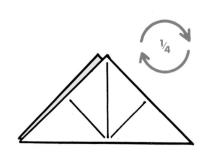

5 You should now have two intersecting valley folds on the white side of your paper. These two creases should look like a plus sign.

6 Turn your paper over to the colored side. The two creases you just looked at should now appear as mountain folds. Position your paper so it appears diamond-shaped. One corner of the square will be nearest to you.

7 Diaper fold: Bring bottom corner up to meet the corner at the top of the diamond. When both corners are precisely aligned, run your hand along the folded edge and make a sharp crease. Your paper should now have the form of a triangle.

8 Rotate your triangle so the folded edge that was at the base is now at the side.

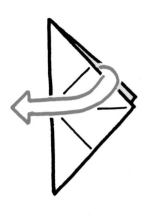 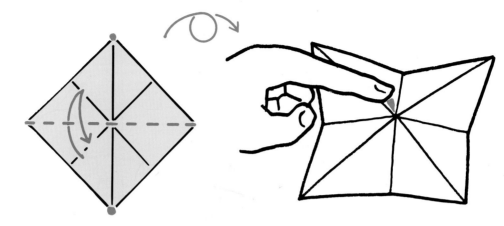

9 Open the triangle.

10 Diaper fold and unfold: You should have a valley fold connecting the top and bottom corners of your diamond shape. Now make a crease connecting the two side corners of the diamond. Bring the bottom corner up to meet the top corner and crease at the base of the triangle. Unfold your paper.

11 Turn the paper back over to white side and position so that one edge is near you. The four creases you have just made should intersect at the center of your square and form a star or Union Jack pattern. Hold your paper loosely, do not flatten. You should be able to see the pattern of the creases that radiate from the center as alternating mountain fold, valley fold, mountain fold, valley fold, etc.

This alternating crease pattern should give your paper a spring, or tension. Place your finger in the very center of the square (where all creases intersect), and push center point down. As you pop in one direction, the four corners of square should pop in opposite direction. Leave center pushed down, and four corners should be pointing up.

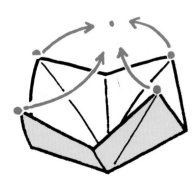 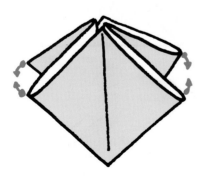 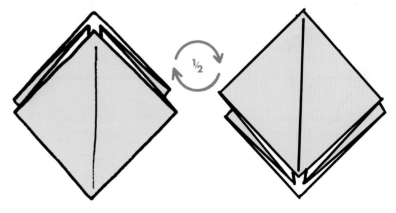

12 Using both hands, push all four corners of square together at same time.

13 Your paper should resemble a flower bud, open on top and closed at the bottom. You should see four flaps extending from the central axis of your model. Flatten the model, bringing two flaps together on each side.

14 Rotate your model so that the closed end is now at the top, and flatten.

15 You should have two flaps at each side of a diamond-shaped square. This is called a preliminary base because it is the basis for making many origami models.

WATERBOMB BASE

The waterbomb base is named after a traditional model called the Waterbomb or Paper Balloon, which starts from this base.

NOTE: The preliminary base and waterbomb base are made from the same creasing pattern; one is the other turned inside out.

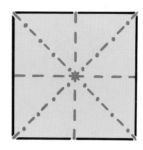

1 Begin as for preliminary base, only start with colored side of paper up.

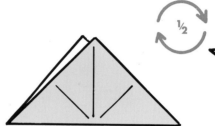

2 Continue through step 10 of preliminary base but leave last diaper fold in place. Rotate paper so that point will be at bottom.

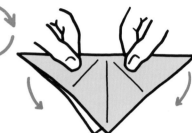

3 This step must be done holding the paper in the air. Lift up diaper fold so that the folded edge is at the top and hold this edge with both hands.

As you push your hands together, the near layer of your paper will pop forward, and the far layer will push back.

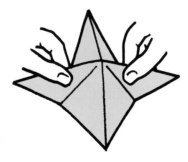

4 (View from top.) You should see four points projecting from the central axis of your model, like a star. Continue to push your hands together as far as you can.

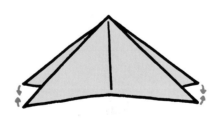

5 Flatten your model so that two flaps rest at each side.

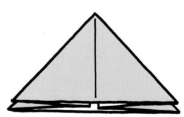

6 Finished waterbomb base. The surface of your model is the shape of a triangle, but if you look under the bottom edge, you will see additional layers of paper.

Umbrella Base

Begin with a preliminary base. Drawing shows side view of preliminary base and inside layers.

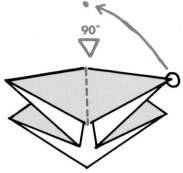

1 Begin to lift up one side flap of your preliminary base as if you were turning the page in a book, but stop when the flap is standing straight up in the air at a right angle to the rest of your model.

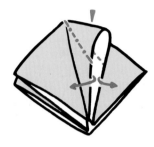

2 Squash fold: Notice that this flap takes the shape of a triangle. One sloping side is a folded edge and one sloping side is a double raw edge that can be opened. As you separate the two raw edges, push down on the folded edge so that it unfolds. What was a triangular flap standing up has now been flattened or squashed into a tall triangle with two small triangle "feet." Down the middle of the tall triangle is a mountain crease where the folded edge had been; make sure this crease runs down the center of your model and connects with the gap you see between the two triangle "feet."

3 When everything is lined up and centered, run your fingers along the sides of the tall triangle and press flat. The move you have just done is called a squash fold.

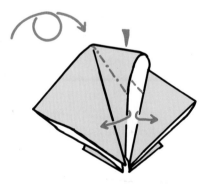

4 Turn your model over and repeat from step 1, squashing another of the flaps from your original preliminary base.

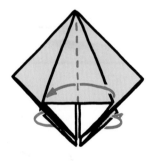

5 You will be squashing all four of the original flaps on the preliminary base. You have already squashed two (front and back); now you need to squash the flaps that are protruding at the sides. Each flap you have already squashed created two half-size flaps. Turn the right half-size flap over to meet the left one as if turning the page of a book. For accurate folding it is important to keep your model balanced (same number of flaps on each side of the central axis). At this point, turn your model over and repeat this step on the back.

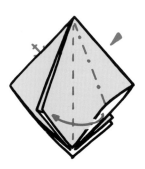  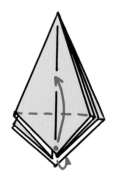 

6 On the right you will now have exposed another full-size flap to squash. Repeat steps 1 through 3 on this flap. Turn over and repeat on back.

7 You should now have eight half-size flaps in total. Be sure your model is balanced—four flaps on each side. Bring the top right flap over to the left (turn the page). Turn your model over and repeat behind.

8 The surface you have just exposed is a solid shape (upside-down kite) with a smooth surface. Lift the bottom point up, front layer only, as far as it will go. Repeat behind.

9 Your tall triangle will now have a smaller triangle sitting at its base. Fold first two flaps on right over to left (turn two pages). Repeat behind.

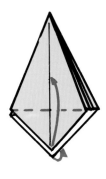  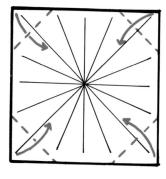 

10 Repeat step 8, front and back.

11 Unfold your model completely. Lay it on table with white side up.

12 At each corner of your square is a triangular shape with a mountain fold at its base. Change this mountain to a valley fold, so that the outside corners (small colored triangles) are turned in and rest on white side of paper. Turn in all four corners of the square.

13 Your paper is now shaped like an octagon. Using the creases already in your paper, re-form it into the tall triangular shape you had before you opened your paper, only now you no longer have a small white triangle showing.

14 When held loosely, it should resemble an umbrella.

15 Flatten your model and make sure it is balanced — four flaps on each side. This is your umbrella base.

BIRD BASE

Begin with preliminary base. Place on table so that closed point is away from you and opening is near you.

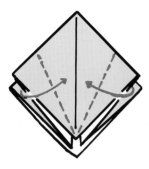

1 You should have two flaps (a front and a back flap) on each side of the preliminary base. Bring the double raw edges from one front flap over to sit on the center line. Repeat on the other front flap.

2 You have made an ice cream cone fold with the front layers of your model. Fold top triangle ("ice cream") down, using top of "cone" as your guide.

3 Leaving triangular flap folded down, unfold ice cream cone creases made in step 1.

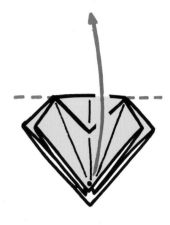

4 There are several layers of paper exposed at bottom of model. Lift up bottom point of front layer only. Swing point all the way up as far as you can—the fold you made when you turned down the "ice cream" will be your guide. (Triangular flap will also swing up.)

5 The front of your model will look like a boat. Bring the long side edges of the boat (raw edges) together so they meet each other and sit on the vertical center line. Make sure the top and bottom points are even. Run your finger around the folded edges to sharpen.

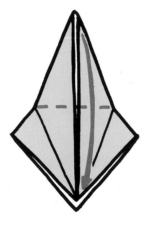

6 Bring the top point down to the bottom of the model.

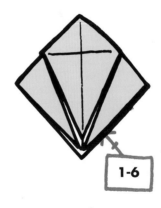

1-6

7 Turn the model over and repeat steps 1 through 6 on the back.

8 This is your completed bird base. It is so called because the traditional Japanese Crane and Flapping Bird as well as many other bird models can be folded from this base. It is the starting point for many other models as well.

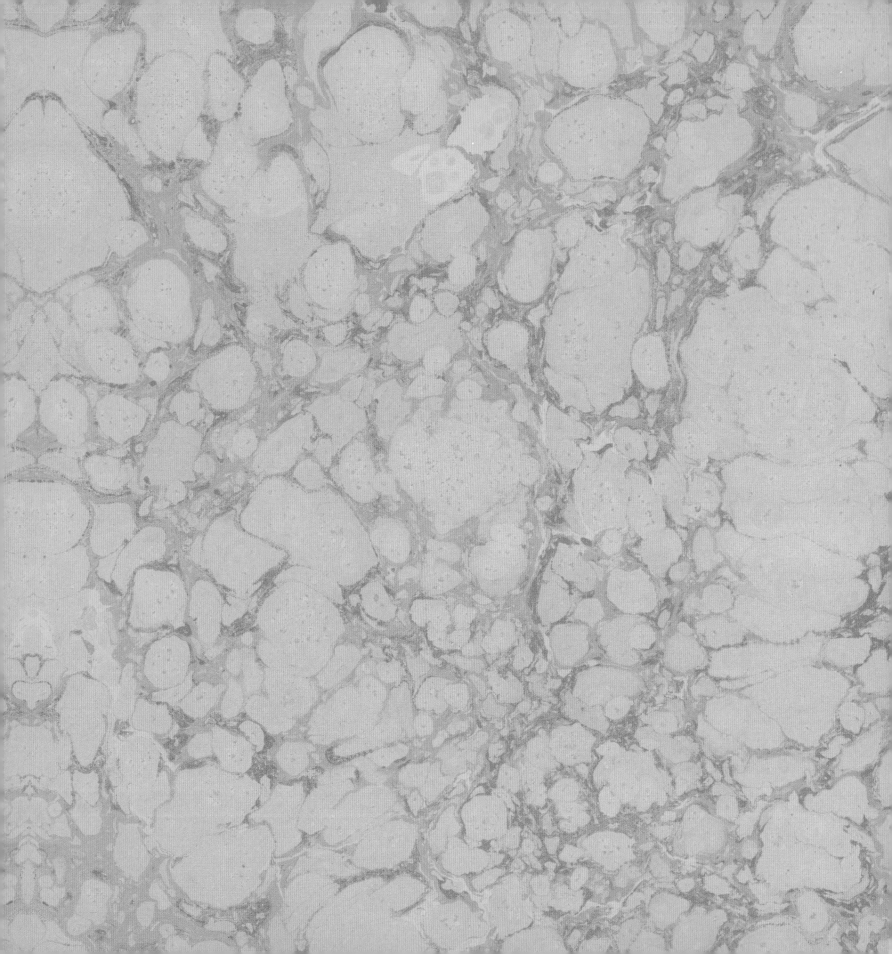

Part II

PAPERFOLDING PROJECTS

The origami projects featured in this book are rated according to their level of difficulty. The following symbols appear with each project:

VERY EASY ▲

EASY ▲▲

INTERMEDIATE ▲▲▲

CHALLENGING ▲▲▲▲

Tricks and Toys

SHIRT AND PANTS

◆

Design by Rachel Katz

▲▲ PAPER: One rectangle in the proportion 2:1 (half a square) for the Shirt and a rectangle of equal size for the Pants.

SHIRT:

1 Begin with the colored side of your rectangle facing up. Pinch the center of each short side of your rectangle.

2 Cupboard fold and unfold: Fold the long sides inward to meet at the center, using your pinch marks as a guide. Crease and unfold.

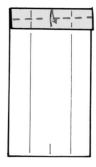

3 Turn your paper over to the white side and position it so that the short sides are at the top and bottom. At the top edge, fold down a colored hem equal in width or slightly narrower than one cupboard door flap.

4 Take the raw edge of the hem and bring it up to the folded edge. Crease and unfold.

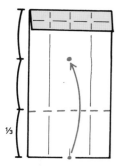

5 Fold the bottom edge up one-third the height of the figure. (Check to make sure your one-third fold is accurate and adjust it if necessary.)

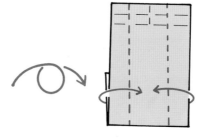

6 Unfold the hem so the top edge is a raw edge again. Then turn your model over to the colored side.

7 Cupboard fold: Fold the longer sides inward to meet at the center. You are folding along existing creases.

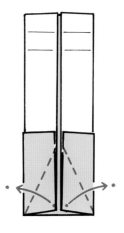

8 Lift the loose corners at the center of the bottom edge and spread them apart. (Notice in the drawing where the slanted folds you are making start and end.)

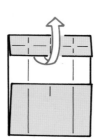

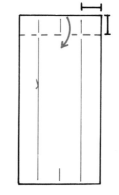

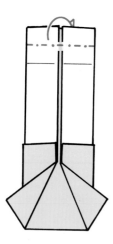

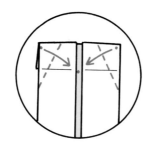

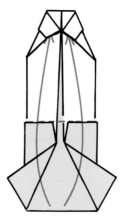

9 Your figure should now look like this. Mountain-fold the top edge to the back, along the existing crease that is the closest to the top edge.

10 Fold the top corners down and inward to meet at the intersection of the horizontal crease and the vertical centerline. You are forming the Shirt's collar.

11 Lift the bottom edge up and slide it under the points of the collar as far as it will comfortably go. Crease firmly at the new bottom edge of your Shirt.

12 Here is your completed Shirt. Notice the opening at the bottom of the Shirt. This is where you will insert the Pants.

VARIATIONS:

You can vary the look of your Shirt by adding a white border to the bottom of the Shirt and the sleeves.

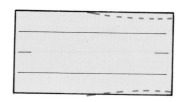

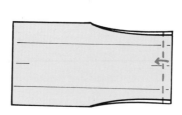

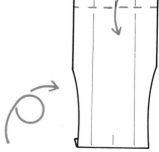

1 Follow steps 1 and 2 for the Shirt. The colored side of your paper is still facing up.

2 To form a border on the sleeves: On half of each of the long edges, fold in a very narrow, tapered hem, as shown in the drawing.

3 To form a border on the Shirt bottom: At the short edge that lies between the hems you just formed, fold in a small hem.

4 Turn your paper over to the all-white side, and continue with step 3 of the Shirt. The hem you just folded in should be at the back side of the bottom edge.

If you would like your Shirt to be white with colored collar and hems, reverse all the color instructions in the diagrams.

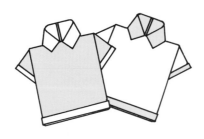

This model can also be folded from money. It is not necessary to have your paper be exactly in the proportion 2:1. Follow the original instructions, leaving out the variation that creates a different colored hem if your currency already has a border on it.

PANTS:

 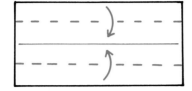  

1 Book fold and unfold: Begin with the white side of your rectangle facing up. Bring the long edges together, folding the paper in half. Crease and unfold.

2 Cupboard fold: Fold the long sides inward to meet at the center.

3 Fold the figure in half again, refolding on the existing crease.

4 Fold the short sides toward each other, but leave them slightly apart as shown in the next drawing.

 # VARIATION:

5 Slide the Pants into the opening at the bottom of your Shirt. You can adjust the length of the Pants' legs by sliding the Pants farther in or out until they look right to you.

To add a white hem at the bottom of your Pants, begin with the colored side of your paper facing up. Fold a small white hem on each short side of your rectangle. Then turn your paper back to the white side and continue with step 1 of the Pants instructions.

Experiment with different-colored and different-patterned papers to vary the look of your Shirt and Pants. See if you can create a Skirt to go with the Shirt by using a square half the size of the rectangle you used for the Shirt. Combine other origami models as accessories. Use your imagination to create a whole fashion line of coordinated outfits.

MAGIC POCKET

Traditional Design

▲ PAPER: One rectangle in the proportion of 2:1
(half a square), such as 10" x 5" (25 x 12.5cm).

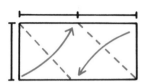

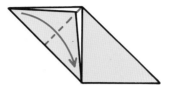

1 Begin with the white side of your rectangle facing up and the long sides at the top and bottom. Fold the left side up to lie along the top edge of your paper. Fold the right side down to lie along the bottom edge.

2 Fold the sharp point at the top left down to touch the bottom of the vertical centerline

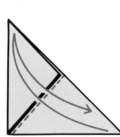

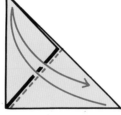

3 Flip the small triangle on the left to the right, folding along the vertical gap.

4 Fold the bottom right point up to the top. Your crease will lie along the folded edge that divides the large triangle in half. Crease sharply and unfold.

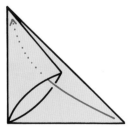

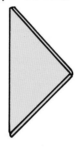

5 Squeeze the smaller, top triangle slightly, causing the double-folded edge to open up into a pocket. Insert the bottom right point into the pocket and slide it in as far as it will go.

6 Here is your completed model. Notice that your model has two separate and identical pockets. Show only one pocket at a time to your audience so they will not realize there are two.

PERFORMING THE TRICK

Secretly fold a one-dollar bill (or any paper currency with a low denomination) and hide it in one pocket. Press that pocket closed. Show the Magic Pocket to your audience. Squeeze open the empty pocket and show them it is empty. Ask to borrow a bill from someone (anything larger than the first bill). Fold it up and insert it in the empty pocket and press it closed. As you talk and move your hand in the air, rotate the model so the other pocket is now facing toward your audience. You can add some magician's flair such as tapping on the model, blowing on it, or saying a magic word. When you open the pocket, the borrowed bill has turned into a bill worth less money!

In a similar manner, you can transform a piece of colored tissue paper into many smaller pieces (prehidden in a pocket) or make whatever flat item you insert disappear.

32

STELLATED OCTAHEDRON

◆

Design by Sam Ciulla

▲▲ PAPER: Almost any size or type of paper will work. You should know the waterbomb base to make this model.

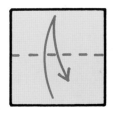

1 Begin with the colored side facing up. Book fold and unfold: fold your paper in half and unfold.

2 Cupboard fold and unfold: bring the top and bottom edges to the horizontal centerline. Crease and unfold.

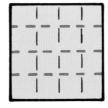

3 Rotate your paper one-quarter turn so that the creases you made are now vertical. Repeat steps 1 and 2 in this direction.

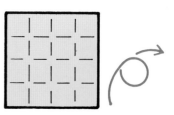

4 Your paper should now be divided into a grid of sixteen little boxes. Turn your paper over to the white side and position it so one corner is near you.

5 Diaper fold and unfold (two times): Bring the bottom corner up to the top corner. Crease and unfold. Rotate your paper one-quarter turn, then crease the other diagonal and unfold.

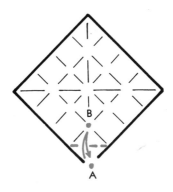

6 Locate the bottom corner (dot A). Then locate on your grid the nearest intersection of creases (dot B). Fold dot A to dot B. Crease and unfold.

7 Locate the second nearest intersection of creases (dot C), which also happens to be the center point of your paper. Fold dot A to dot C. Crease and unfold.

◆

WHAT IS A STELLATED OCTAHEDRON?

Most people know that an octagon is a two-dimensional shape having eight sides. An octahedron is a three-dimensional shape having eight faces. "Stellated" refers to the fact that each face of the shape points outward instead of being flat, giving it a stellar, or starlike, appearance.

◆

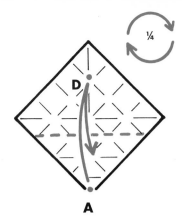
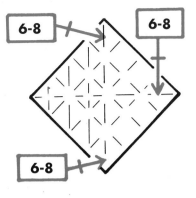

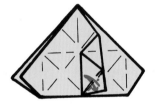
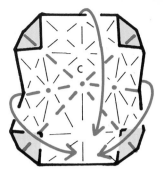

8 Locate the farthest intersection of creases (dot D). Fold dot A to dot D. Crease and unfold.

9 Rotate your paper one-quarter turn. The new bottom corner now becomes dot A. Repeat steps 6 through 8 three more times.

10 The result should be a grid of sixteen little boxes with an X in the center of each box. Blunt the corners of your paper by folding each outside corner in along the nearest crease.

11 Press down at C to make the center point pop away from you. Raise the sides along the existing mountain folds and push the sides toward each other and down to the center of the bottom edge. Flatten the model. The result is a waterbomb base with blunted corners.

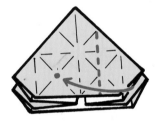
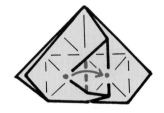
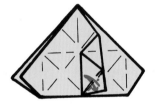

12 Notice the two small boxes that lie on the bottom edge of your paper; each has an X in the center. Bring the far right corner (front layer only) past the nearest X to the center of the second X.

13 Bring the same corner back to touch the folded edge you created in step 12.

14 In step 13, you created a triangular flap. Look for the smaller triangular flap that lies along the lower edge of this one. Fold the smaller triangular flap upward. Crease firmly and unfold.

15 Put your finger inside the pocket formed by the double edge at the lower edge of the large triangular flap. Remove your finger, squeeze the pocket open, and insert the smaller triangular flap into this pocket.

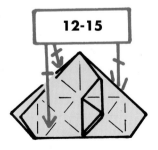

16 Repeat steps 12 through 15 on the left side of your model. Then turn your paper over and repeat on the back.

17 Slightly separate the top and bottom layers of paper and blow into the opening to inflate the ball.

18 Within each diamond shape on your ball, find the valley fold and gently press inward with a finger to give the ball a faceted look.

Action Toy: Place the model on the table so that the opening is at the top. Release the ball and it will roll over for you.

See page 103 for instructions on hanging origami models.

GYROSCOPE

◆

Design by Lewis Simon

▲▲ PAPER: Twelve squares of equal size. Approximately 3" (7.5cm) square is a good size. Foil paper works well because the slippery quality of its foil side helps the units slide together at the end. Origami paper or other lightweight paper can also be used.

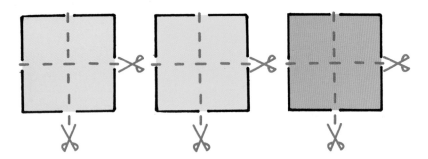

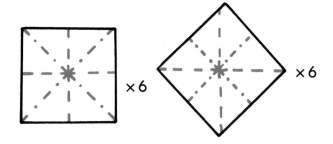

1 If you do not have twelve small squares, use three 6"
(15cm) squares and cut each into quarters.

2 Fold six of your squares into preliminary bases.

Fold the other six into waterbomb bases.

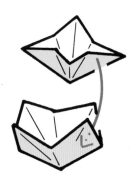

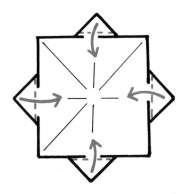

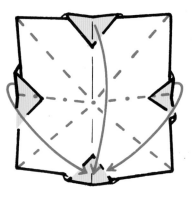

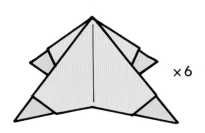

3 Half-open one preliminary base and one waterbomb base and lay them on the table, white sides facing up. Place the waterbomb base over the preliminary base so that their mountain and valley creases match each other.

4 Find the corners of the preliminary base (the lower layer) that extend out beyond the edges of the waterbomb base. Turn these corners over the edges of the waterbomb base, forming little colored triangles. Make your fold a thick hair's width away from the raw edge of the paper. This slight gap will help you later when you join the units together.

5 Reclose the preliminary and waterbomb bases and you have completed one unit.

6 Repeat steps 3 through 5 with the remaining preliminary and waterbomb bases to give you a total of six completed units.

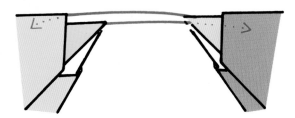

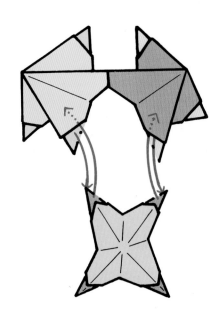

7 Assembly: each unit has four small triangular-shaped tabs protruding out at the ends; slightly separate the raw edges of a tab from one unit and fit it over the mountain-folded edge of a tab from a second unit; slide the units together so that the two tabs are completely hidden.

8 Take a third unit and join two of its tabs to a free tab on each of the first two units.

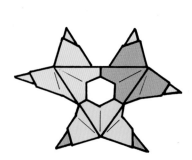

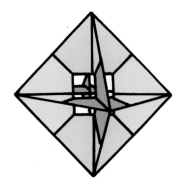

9 Notice the triangular outline you have created by joining the three units. Keep adding more units in a similar manner to complete the structure of your Gyroscope. Don't get discouraged with your last unit; in modulars, these are always the hardest to add.

10 Use your completed Gyroscope as a decoration, or hold it between two open palms and blow.

MAGIC STAR

◆

Design by Robert Neale

▲▲ PAPER: Eight squares of equal size, each approximately 3" (7.5cm) square. Foil paper, origami paper, or similar lightweight paper works well.

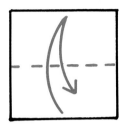

1 Book fold and unfold: begin with one square, white side facing up. Fold your square in half and unfold.

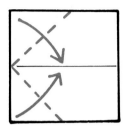

2 House-roof fold: fold the top and bottom left corners inward to meet at the horizontal centerline. Your paper will resemble a sideways house.

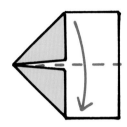

3 Fold in half along the existing horizontal crease.

This modular design is made from eight identical units linked together with a folded lock. To vary the look of your finished model, try experimenting with different color patterns:

8 different colors
(1 square of each color)
4 different colors
(2 squares of each color)
2 different colors
(4 squares of each color)

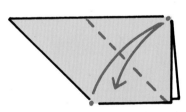

4 Fold the top right corner down so that the side raw edges lie on the bottom raw edges. Make a very sharp crease and unfold. Press your finger over the crease you just made to flatten it.

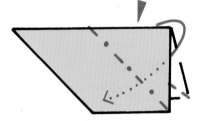

5 Inside reverse fold: slightly separate the front and back layers. Push down on the right side of the top folded edge, inserting this edge in between the front and back layers. The creases you made in step 4 will now become folded edges.

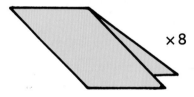

×8

6 Flatten the paper and you have your finished unit. Notice the two "arms" you have formed on the right. Repeat steps 1 through 5 with the remaining squares to give you a total of eight units.

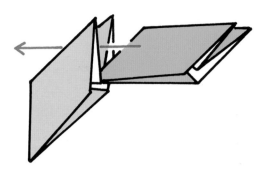

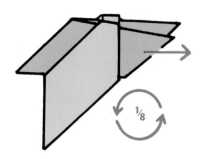

7 Study the drawing careful-ly and hold two units as shown: the arms of the first unit are pointing up; the arms of the second unit are at the right. Slide the second unit between the arms of the first. The second unit should sit flush against the inner groove of the first unit.

8 Wrap the protruding tips of unit one around the arms of unit two to lock the units togeth-er. Be careful to make these folds very neat but not too tight or your finished model will buckle.

9 Slide the second unit as far to the right as the lock will allow and check to make sure you have a smooth sliding action. Then rotate your model slightly so the open arms of the second unit are now pointing up.

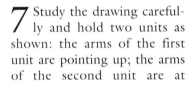
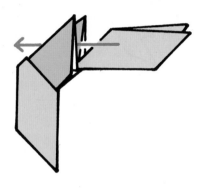
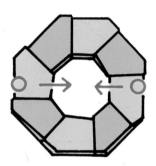
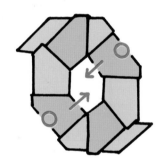

10 Hold the third unit with the arms at the right and slide it between the arms of the second unit. Make sure it sits flush against the inner groove of unit two.

11 Lock them together as you did the first two units and then slide the third unit to the right. Continue adding units until all eight are joined together. The last unit will join with the first to form a full circle.

12 The completed ring. To transform your ring into a star: hold the ring at opposite sides and gently push your hands together as far as the ring will comfortably allow.

Rotate the model slightly and again push your hands gently together. Continue in this man-ner until the star pattern is formed.

To transform back to a ring: hold on to the inner pattern at opposite sides of your star and pull gently apart until you are stopped by the lock in the paper. Rotate the model slightly and pull from this new position. Continue repositioning your fin-gers and pulling until you have a ring again.

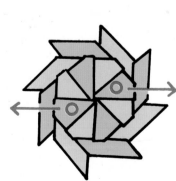
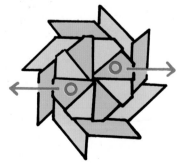

To send a greeting: write a greeting on the points of the star. When you open the model out to a ring, the message will disappear. When you give some-one the ring, show them how to transform it into a star and the message will reappear.

KALEIDOSCOPE FLOWER

◆

Collected by Fumio Inoue and Hisa Amimoto

▲▲▲ PAPER: Seven squares, each approximately 4" (10cm) square, preferably in several different colors.
Use origami paper, foil paper, gift wrap, or duo paper (a different color on each side).

THE SPRING UNIT:

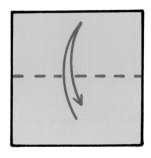 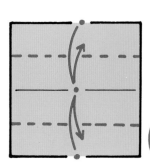 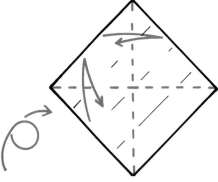 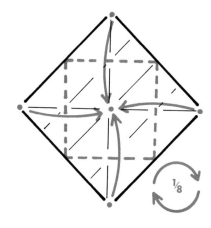

1 Begin with a square, colored side up. Book fold and unfold: bring the bottom edge up to the top edge. Crease and unfold.

2 Cupboard fold and unfold: bring the top and bottom edges inward to meet at the centerline, crease, and unfold.

3 Turn your paper over to the white side and position it so that one corner is near you. Diaper fold and unfold (two times): fold and unfold your paper along each diagonal.

4 Blintz fold: bring each outside corner inward to meet at the center point of your square.

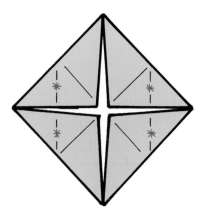  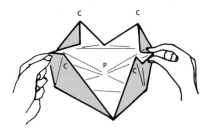 

5 Position the paper as shown (notice the short vertical creases [marked with an asterisk] at the sides).

6 Pick your paper up in the air. As you pinch the side corners in half with a mountain fold...

7 ...let corners C pop up at you as center point P on the underneath layer pops down. (Note: you are not making any new creases but using the existing creases to collapse the model into the shape shown in the following drawings.)

8 Side view of move in progress.

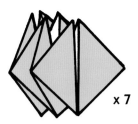

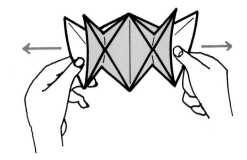

9 Finished spring unit. Use your six remaining squares to make a total of seven identical units. Flatten each unit to sharpen the creases.

10 Insert your thumbs into the bottom of the slits on the front and back of one unit. Then pull your hands out

to the sides, which will spread the unit into a half-open position as shown in the next drawing. Repeat with all seven units.

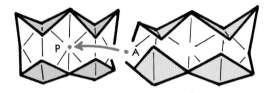

11 Make sure you see vertical creases in each unit. Find the centerpoint of the first unit.

Lay the second unit over the right half of the first so that side point A touches center point P.

12 Continue joining all seven units in a like manner,

always laying the new unit over the right half of the previous unit.

ASSEMBLING THE KALEIDOSCOPE FLOWER:

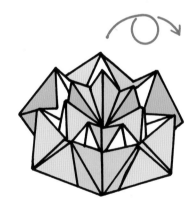

13 When all seven units are loosely joined, neatly reclose the units, making sure all valley and mountain folds are aligned. Squeeze the entire length of joined units together as if you were squeezing an accordion.

14 Release your chain of linked units. Slightly open the last unit on the right, then bend the entire chain into a circle, bringing the end units toward each other.

15 Carefully fit the left unit into the half-opened right unit so that the side point of the left unit lies over the center point of the right unit. When the two units are aligned, reclose them together to complete the ring. This is a difficult step, so have patience and keep trying.

16 This view shows the bottom of your completed Kaleidoscope Flower. Turn it over...

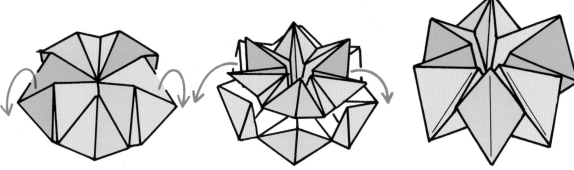

17 ...and gently push the outer edges of the ring backward.

18 Continue pushing until the ring turns completely inside out...

19 ...and you are back to where you started.

Note: if any of the units come apart as you are rotating the ring, you may want to use a drop of glue to hold them together.

JACK-IN-THE-BOX

◆

Design by Nick Robinson

▲▲▲ **PAPER**: Jack's head and arms—one square, 4 ¹/₈" (10.6cm). Jack's "spring" body—five squares, 3" (7.5cm). Box—one square, 8 ¹/₂" (21.5cm). Lid—one square, 6" (15cm).

If you want to make a larger or smaller model, determine the size of paper for Jack as follows:

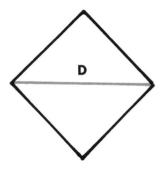

Square used for body

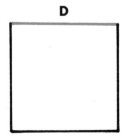

Square used for head and arms

Diagonal of body squares (D)= length of side of head/arms square

JACK'S HEAD AND ARMS

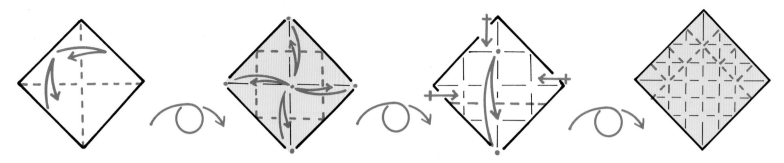

1 Diaper fold and unfold (two times): with the white side facing up, fold and unfold along both diagonals. Turn over to the colored side.

2 Blintz fold and unfold: bring each outside corner to the center point. Crease and unfold. Turn over to the white side.

3 Match the dots: bring the bottom corner up to the farthest crease. Crease and unfold. Rotate paper and repeat step on the other corners.

4 Turn the model back to the colored side. Make the creases shown in the drawing.

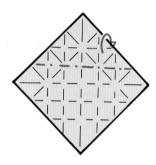

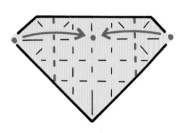

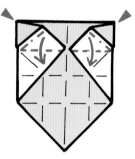

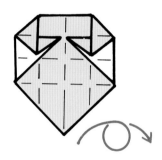

5 Mountain-fold backward on the existing crease above the horizontal centerline.

6 On the existing creases, fold the right and left side corners to the vertical centerline.

7 Push down at the top corners, squashing down along the creases shown to give you the form of drawing 8.

8 Notice the two sharp points that meet at the vertical centerline. These arms will flip out to the sides in the next step. Turn your model over.

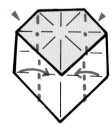

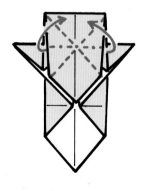

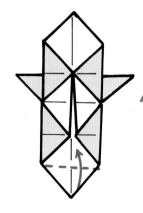

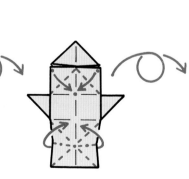

9 Press inward at the small colored edges. As you inside-reverse-fold along the creases shown, allow the arms from the back to swing out to the sides (see the next drawing).

10 On the front layer: folding along the existing waterbomb-base creases, push in at the sides of the horizontal crease and swing the loose point up to the top.

11 Fold up the bottom tip of the model. Turn the model over.

12 At the bottom: make the diagonal creases shown, then collapse the model into a waterbomb base.

At the top: fold the corners down as for a house-roof fold.

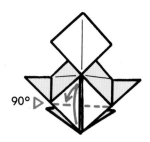

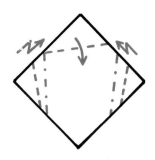

13 Turn back to the front of the model. Make a valley fold at Jack's waist. Crease and unfold halfway. The next drawings show the head only.

14 Head: fold the top corner down to form hair; pleat the side corners to form ears.

15 Mountain-fold the top corners to give the head a rounder shape.

16 Pull down slightly on the loose bottom point but retain the waterbomb base shape below the waist. Jack's head and arms are finished and ready to be joined to the body.

JACK'S BODY:

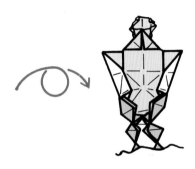

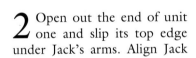

1 Make and join five spring units by following steps 1 through 13 of the Kaleidoscope Flower (see pages 42–43).

2 Open out the end of unit one and slip its top edge under Jack's arms. Align Jack

and the body so that all mountain and valley folds match.

3 Reclose the units so that Jack is securely joined to the body and standing up.

THE BOX:

Fold the square into a cube-shaped box as described on page 60 (instructions for box variations, making a deeper box).

THE LID:

Fold the square into a Masu Box according to the instructions on page 56.

ASSEMBLY:

Glue or tape the bottom of Jack's spring body to the bottom of the cube box. Compress Jack's body and push him down into the box. As you hold Jack down with one finger, cover the box with the lid. Coach Jack out of the box by humming the tune to "Pop! Goes the Weasel." When you get to the "Pop!" part of the song, remove the lid and watch Jack jump out!

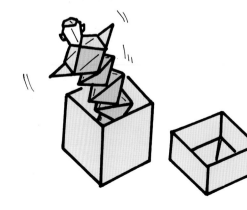

Boxes and Containers

FLOWERPOT

◆

A traditional Spanish design, also created by Florence Temko

▲▲▲ **PAPER:** Most varieties of paper will work well with this model. Almost any size square, 6" (15cm) and larger, can be used. Note—use same size paper you use for Cactus Plant. If Flowerpot is to hold Tulips, use a sheet approximately 10" (25cm) square.

1 Begin with umbrella base. Your umbrella base has eight flaps and eight side corners, one at the outside of each flap. Make sure your model is balanced—four flaps on each side. Bring the side corner of both front flaps up so that bottom edges meet at center line. Turn over and repeat behind.

2 Swing front-side point at right over to left. Turn over and repeat behind.

3 On front layer, bring right- and left-side points up to center. Turn over and repeat behind.

4 All eight side points have now been folded up. Unfold all eight points (two on front, two on back, and four on inside layers).

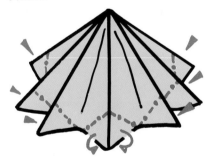   

5 Loosely open out the bottom of the umbrella base and spread flaps apart. On existing creases, reverse-fold one side point inside model. Repeat on the other seven points.

6 Flatten model in a balanced position—four flaps on each side. On the front layer, lift the bottom point up as far as you can. Turn over and repeat behind.

7 Lift front right-side flap and fold over to left (turn one page of book). Turn over and repeat behind.

8 Repeat steps 6 and 7 until all the bottom points have been turned up. (Remember to always keep the model balanced—same number of flaps on each side.)

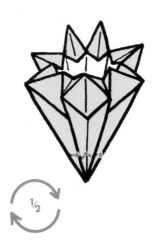

9 Fold the top point down to touch the top of the small triangle. Crease hard and unfold. This crease determines the height of the Flowerpot. If you would like a shallower pot, fold the point farther down.

½

10 To open Flowerpot: spread the side flaps as wide apart as possible. Insert a finger of one hand into the opening. With the other hand push the bottom point up. By pinching between two fingers, reinforce as mountain folds the creases that outline the base of the pot.

11 Finished Flowerpot. When using the Flowerpot to hold origami flowers, you may want to weigh down the bottom by adding pennies or sand.

Bowl

♦

Design by Aldo Putignano

▲▲▲ **PAPER:** Wallpaper, a colorful shopping bag, or foil paper. You'll need a square approximately 10" to 18" (26 to 45cm). Start with the white side up.

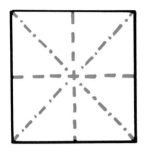

1 Put in creases to make a preliminary base by following steps 1 to 10. Do not close up into preliminary base; leave the paper open, white side facing up.

2 Blintz fold: fold each corner to center of square.

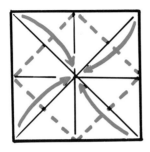

3 Fold top point down to bottom point.

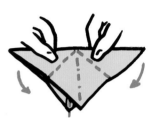

4 Using both hands, hold model at top edge. Push hands together and form model into a waterbomb base with two flaps on each side. (This is called a blintzed waterbomb base because the blintz fold you made in step 2 adds an extra layer inside your model.)

5 Rotate your model so that top point is now at bottom of model.

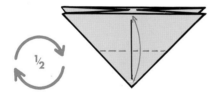

6 Fold bottom point up to center of top edge.

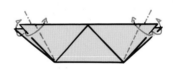

7 Front layer only, fold slanted folded edges toward center—crease should originate where slanted side edge meets bottom folded edge. Repeat behind.

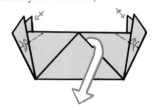

8 Unfold bottom fold. You now have four tabs protruding up. Fold both front tabs down at an angle so that folded edge lies along itself. Crease and unfold. Turn over and repeat behind.

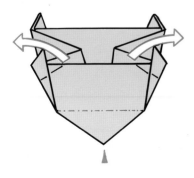

9 Open model from top, leaving protruding tabs in place. Flatten model at bottom using existing creases as your guide.

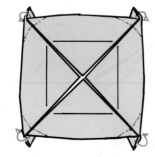

10 (View inside model.) At each corner, mountain-fold point back, using existing creases.

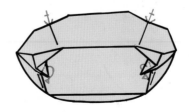

11 (View from side of model.) At each corner of the bowl, mountain-fold point back and tuck into pocket behind it.

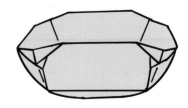

12 Finished Bowl.

A Deeper Bowl:

 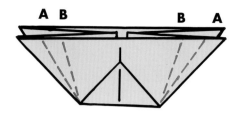

At step 6, fold bottom point up so that it lies on the center line, but below the top edge. The lower you bring the point, the deeper your Bowl will be. Bear in mind that the shorter the length of the new folded edge at the bottom, the less of a base your Bowl will have to sit on. The sides of the Bowl can also be varied by changing the angle at which you fold the sides in at step 7. The nearer to the center you bring the side points, the steeper the sides of the Bowl will be. After you have folded up one side, use it as a guide to make sure the other corners are folded in at the same angle. Choose angle A or angle B, or anywhere in between.

PRACTICAL PURSE

◆

Design by Gay Merrill Gross

▲▲▲ **PAPER:** Wrapping paper, foil paper, or bond paper. You can create a pattern on bond paper by photocopying a small geometric pattern onto paper. This model is especially attractive when duo paper is used, or two different-colored sheets are folded together. Use a square, any size. Approximately 8½" (22cm) square makes a practical-sized purse. The side facing up now will be the color of the inside (lining) of the purse.

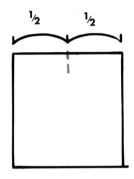

1 Pinch center of top edge.

2 Cupboard-fold and unfold: Using pinch mark as a guide, bring left-and right-side edges to meet at center. Open.

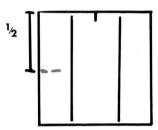

3 Pinch ½ mark on one side edge.

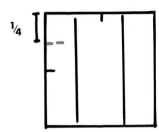

4 Bring top edge to ½ mark and pinch side edge, creating ¼ pinch.

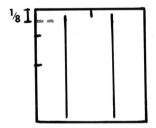

5 Bring top edge to ¼ mark and pinch side edge, creating ⅛ pinch.

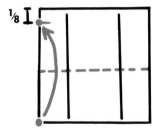

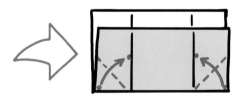

6 Bring bottom edge to ⅛ mark. Crease folded edge all of the way across.

7 Fold up bottom corners so that folded edges lie along the vertical cupboard creases you made in step 2.

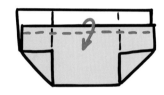

8 On the front layer, fold down horizontal raw edge to create a narrow strip or small hem.

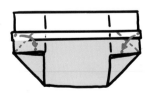

9 Bring corners at end of hem down so that side raw edges of front layer lie along upper edges of triangular flaps—leave a small gap between edges.

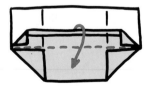

10 Bring folded edge of hem as far down as it will go—you will be creating a fold that runs through the gap between upper and lower triangles.

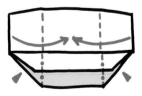

11 Pull upper folded edge of front layer slightly forward to separate front layers from back layer of model. Push inward at slanted folded edges near bottom

of model so that they reverse fold inside model. You will also be folding on existing vertical cupboard creases as side raw edges fold in and meet at center.

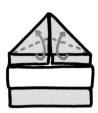

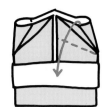

12 House-roof fold: fold top corners down so that each half of the double raw edge at top of model lies along vertical center line.

13 Fold up bottom edges of "roof" to lie along top sloped edges of roof.

14 Slightly unfold last fold and house-roof fold.

15 On right side, grasp mountain fold that juts out and pull down (front layer only) until you have the form of a large colored triangle with a smaller white triangle protruding out from under the raw edge (see next drawing).

16 Repeat step 15 on left side. As you pull down on the mountain folded edge, insert protruding small white triangle under raw edge of right side.

17 Using existing crease, mountain-fold lower triangular area behind itself to lock.

18 Bring top point down to bottom of model.

19 Fold point at bottom of triangular flap backward (mountain fold), and tuck point up into pocket behind it.

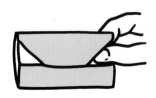

20 Purse is locked. To open, slip finger under top flap and pull up.

21 Open Purse. Use to hold coins, pins, tissues, pills, buttons, sewing kit, business cards, or other items.

Masu Box

◆

Traditional Design

▲▲ **PAPER**: A square of origami paper, foil paper, or wrapping paper is acceptable for smaller boxes. For sturdier boxes, use heavier paper such as bond paper, marbleized paper, wallpaper, decorative shopping bags, or covers from magazines cut into squares. Each side of your finished box will be approximately one-third the length of your original square. The height of the box will be approximately one-sixth the size of the starting square.

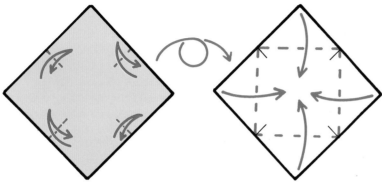 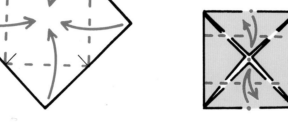 

1 Begin with the colored side of the square facing up. Book fold and unfold (twice): fold and unfold the square in half in both directions. If you do not want these creases to show on your finished box, crease only near the side edges of the square and leave the middle uncreased. Each long "pinch" should be approximately one-fourth the length of one side.

2 Turn your paper over to the white side. Blintz fold: use the creases from step 1 as a guide to fold all four corners to the center.

3 Cupboard fold and unfold: bring the top and bottom edges inward to meet at the center. Crease sharply and unfold.

4 Cupboard fold and unfold: bring the right and left sides inward to meet at the center. Crease sharply and unfold.

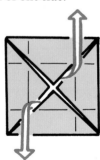 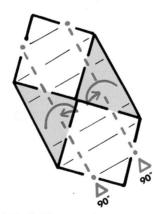 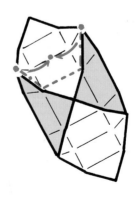 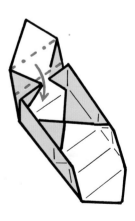

5 Unfold the top and bottom triangular flaps.

6 Refold on the existing creases that connect the far dots. Crease sharply and then partially unfold so that the two flaps stand at a right angle to the rest of the model. They form two sides of your box.

7 For this step you will be folding simultaneously on three existing creases: push inward on the small mountain-fold creases where the color and white meet. At the same time, valley-fold on the crease that connects these two mountain folds.

8 You should now have formed the third side of your box. Grasp the long tab that sticks up and pull it down and inside the box so that it lines the inside of the box.

56

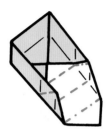

9 Repeat steps 7 and 8 on the other open end of your box.

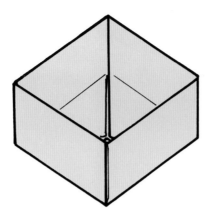

10 Reinforce the creases on the finished box.

OPTIONAL BOX "TRICKS":

•To keep the four flaps that line the inside of your box from "popping" up, lift the flaps up for a moment and place a small piece of tape, sticky side up, in the center of the box. Replace the flaps so that they stick to the tape and also cover it so it is hidden from view.

•For an extra-sturdy box, cut a piece of cardboard to fit in the bottom. Unfold the box back to step 7 and insert the cardboard under the two bottom flaps. Then refold the box and the cardboard will be hidden.

Box Cover

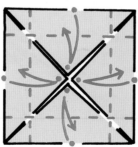

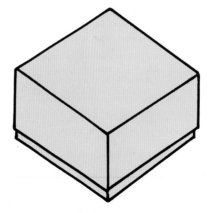

Use a square the same size as the square you used for the Masu Box. Follow the instructions for the box but replace steps 3 and 4 with the following:

3 and **4** Fold the bottom edge up to lie approximately $1/8$" (0.3cm) below the center. (The size of the gap may vary from $1/16$" to $3/16$" (0.2 to 0.4cm) depending on the thickness of the paper you are using.) Crease sharply and unfold. Repeat on all four sides of the blintzed square. Continue from step 5 of the box.

Fit the finished cover over the box.

Box Divider

◆

Design by Paolo Bascetta

▲ ▲ **PAPER:** A square the same size as the square you used for folding the Box.

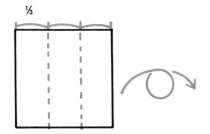

⅓

1 With the white side facing up, fold your square into thirds, then turn it over to the colored side.

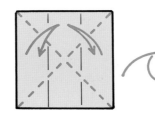

2 Diaper fold and unfold (twice): Fold your paper in half along both diagonals, then turn it back to the white side and position your paper so that the creases made in step 1 are vertical.

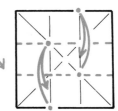

3 Divide the model in thirds: bring the bottom edge to the farthest intersection of creases (match dot to dot). Crease and unfold. Repeat with the top edge.

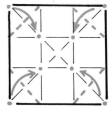

4 Fold each outside corner to the nearest intersection of creases.

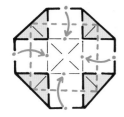

5 Fold each raw edge to the nearest crease.

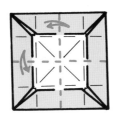

6 Book fold and unfold (twice): fold the model in half in both directions. Then turn the model over.

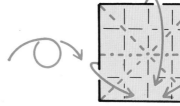

7 Using the existing creases, collapse your paper into a waterbomb base.

8 Lift the bottom edge (of the front layer only) to the top point of the model. This will form the three-dimensional shape shown in the next drawing.

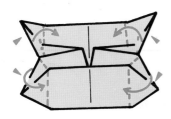

9 Gently push the outside points inward to form the model into the two rectangular box shapes shown in the next drawing.

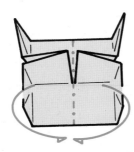

10 Mountain-fold the model in half down the vertical centerline. The result is...

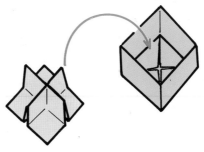

11 ...a plus-sign standing on top of four little squares. This is your finished Box Divider.

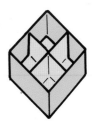

12 Insert the divider into the box. Add a cover if you wish.

BOX VARIATIONS

DEEP OR SHALLOW BOX

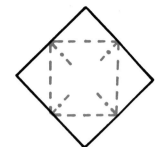

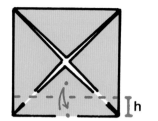

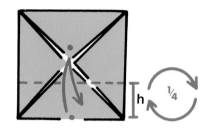

You can vary the height of your box by varying the amount you fold the sides inward after the paper is folded into a blintz fold.

1 Follow steps 1 and 2 for the Masu Box.

2 To make a shallower box: fold the bottom edge up to a spot below the center. (Distance h equals the height of your finished box.) Crease sharply and unfold. Rotate your paper one-quarter turn.

To make a deeper box: fold the bottom edge past the center (but not more than one-third the length of the present size of your paper.) Crease sharply and unfold. Rotate your paper one-quarter turn.

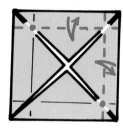

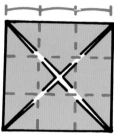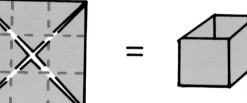

3 Using intersection point A as a guide, fold the bottom edge up an equal amount as in step 2. Crease sharply and unfold.

4 Repeat step 3 on the remaining two sides of your square.

Note: If you fold your paper in thirds in steps 2 though 4, your finished box will be the shape of a cube.

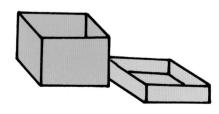

5 Continue from step 5 of the Masu Box.

Your completed shallow and deep boxes will look similar to these. Experiment with different-size papers to see if you can make a shallow box to fit as a lid on a deep box.

RECTANGULAR BOX

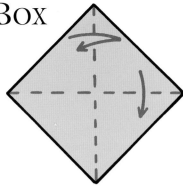

All of the box variations we have made thus far have square bottoms. Here's how to vary the same box so that it has a rectangular bottom.

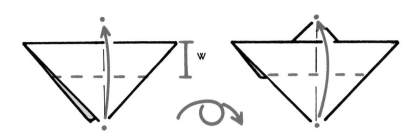

1 Begin with the colored side facing up. Diaper-fold and unfold in both directions. Leave in the second diaper fold.

2 Fold one bottom corner up past the top edge of the paper. (Distance W will be the width of your finished box.) Turn over.

3 Make sure the vertical centerline creases are aligned. Then fold up the bottom corner to match the top corner. (If you are making a lid for your box, take a second sheet of paper and follow steps 1 through 3, making sure distance W is the same on both sheets.)

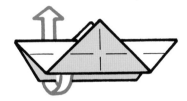

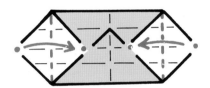

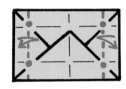

4 Bring the bottom folded edge (front layer only) up to the long folded edge. Crease sharply and unfold. Turn the paper over and repeat. (For a box lid: bring the bottom folded edge up to slightly below the long folded edge.)

5 Unfold the horizontal mountainfold. The two top points will cross each other on the flattened paper.

6 Fold the right and left side corners inward to the nearest intersection of raw edges and you will completely cover the white.

7 Connect the dots: fold the right and left side edges inward, making a valley fold that connects the points marked (the intersection of the raw edges and the crease). Crease sharply and unfold.

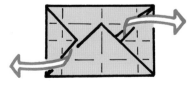

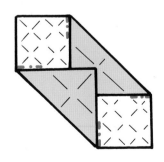

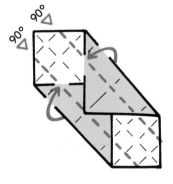

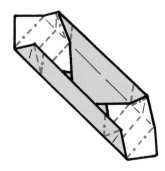

8 Unfold the triangular flaps back out to the sides.

9 Pinch mountain folds where shown in the drawing.

10 Fold the long sides up to stand at a right angle to the rest of the paper. This will form two sides of your box.

11 Form the last two sides in the same manner as for the Masu Box.

12 Completed Rectangular Box.

CARD CASE

Design by Humiaki Huzita

▲ **PAPER:** Use a sheet of A4 or 8½" x 11" letter-size paper (21.5 x 28cm).

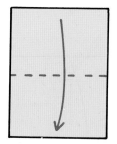

1 If your paper has a color or pattern on only one side, begin with that side facing up. Bring the short top edge down to meet the short bottom edge, folding the paper in half.

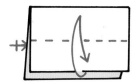

2 Bring the bottom raw edge (front layer only) up to the top folded edge. Crease and unfold. Turn over and repeat on the other side.

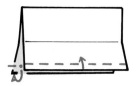

3 On the front layer, fold the bottom raw edge up approximately ½" (1.5cm) to create a small hem. Then turn your model to the back and fold up a matching hem on the back layer.

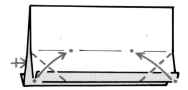

4 On the front layer, fold the bottom corners up to the horizontal crease. Turn the model over and repeat.

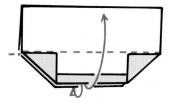

5 On the front layer, refold on the existing horizontal crease. Repeat on the other side.

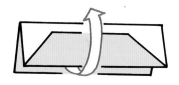

6 Unfold the folded edge.

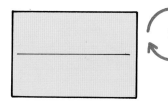

7 Rotate your paper one-quarter turn, so the short edges are at the top and bottom.

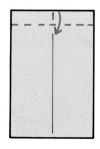

8 Fold down the top edge to form a hem approximately 1" (2.5cm) wide.

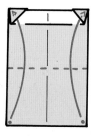

9 Notice the two triangular pockets at either side of the hem. Bring the bottom edge upward and insert its corners into the triangular pockets. Slide the bottom edge as far up as it will comfortably fit inside the pockets and then make a firm crease along the new bottom edge.

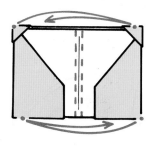

10 Fold the left side of the model over to almost touch the right side, leaving a small gap. Crease firmly, then unfold. Repeat, bringing the right side almost to the left. These two folds form the spine of your case.

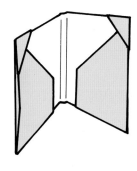

11 Your case is now complete. You will find four pockets for holding cards, two on the outside and two on the inside.

Card Case Variations

Picture Frame Case

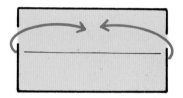

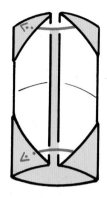

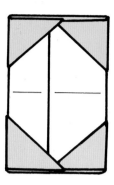

1 Follow steps 1 through 6 of the Card Case. Bend the short sides of the model toward each other.

2 Slip the corners of one end into the pockets of the other end. Slide the two ends together until the model is a little wider than the size of the card or other item you wish it to hold. Press down firmly on the folded sides.

3 Form a spine for the case as you did in step 10 of the original Card Case. Or leave the model flat without a spine and use it as a picture frame.

PORTFOLIO

You can fold either the Card Case or Picture Frame Case design from larger paper to use as a portfolio for holding larger items. Suggested folding papers include marbleized paper, a poster, a map, fadeless paper, or kraft paper.

- **To make a case to hold 6" (15cm) origami paper, start with a sheet 16" x 27" (41 x 69cm).**
- **To make a portfolio for letter-size paper, use a sheet 28" x 40" (70 x 100cm).**

Card or Photo Holder

Design by Ralph Matthews

▲ **PAPER:** Two rectangles of equal size in the proportion 2:1. A 6" (15cm) or smaller square can be cut in half to give you two rectangles.

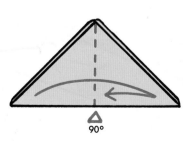

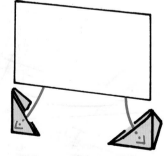

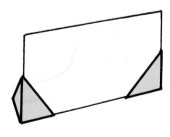

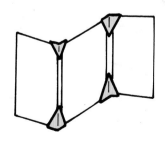

1 Fold each rectangle into a Magic Pocket (see page 32). Fold each model in half. Crease sharply and partially unfold the last crease.

2 Stand the models on a table as shown and insert your card or photo into one pocket of each model.

3 Here is your completed Card Holder.

Use several small corner hinges to join photographs for display.

Plants, Animals, and Birds

CRANE

◆

Traditional Design

▲▲▲ **PAPER**: Lightweight paper such as origami paper, foil paper, or gift wrap. Paper of any size can be used, but 6" (15cm) square is recommended for your first attempts. As a challenge, some people have folded cranes from squares less than ¹/₂" (1.3cm) in size!

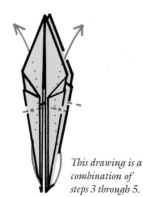

This drawing is a combination of steps 3 through 5.

1 Begin with a bird base (page 25). Make sure the split in the diamond shape is pointing toward you. Fold the lower edges (front layer only) inward to almost touch the vertical centerline. Turn the model over and repeat.

2 The two points at the top of the model are wings. The two sharp "spikes" at the bottom will be inside-reverse-folded up and between the wings to become a neck and a tail. To simplify the inside reverse fold...

3 ...turn the page: fold the front layer at the right over to the left, as if turning the page of a book.

4 Lift the bottom point up to the top.

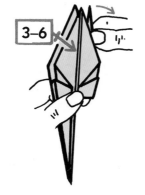

5 Turn the left page (front layer only) back to the right. As you do so the "spike" will be sandwiched in between the wings.

6 Before you flatten the front and back layers, pull the "spike" slightly out to the side and set it in this position by pinching the base of the wing. Repeat steps 3 through 6 on the left.

7 Inside-reverse-fold the tip of one slender point to form a head.

8 Spread the wings apart.

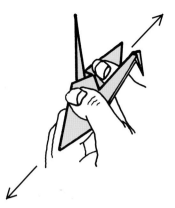

9 Hold each wing close to the central triangle. Gently pull your hands apart, causing the triangle to spread and flatten.

10 The Crane is finished. In Japanese culture, a garland of one thousand cranes represents an especially strong wish for good health. To make the garland, the cranes are usually left with their wings up (the position of the model in step 8). They are then strung on threads, one on top of the other. These same garlands are made by schoolchildren all over the world and sent to be draped across the memorial statue of Sadako Sasaki at the Hiroshima Peace Park.

CHAIN OF CRANES

◆━━━━━━━━━━━━━━━━━━━━

Thomas Hull's variation on a traditional design

▲▲▲ **PAPER:** Two or more squares of equal size.

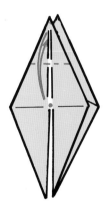

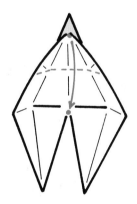

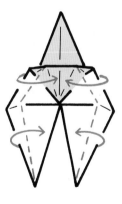

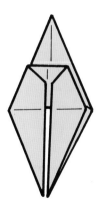

1 Begin with a bird base (see page 25). Fold one top point down to the horizontal center of the model. Crease sharply and unfold.

2 Separate the long raw edges of the diamond and again fold the top point down to the middle. Sharply crease the horizontal folded edge at the top of the triangle you have folded down. Extend this crease out to the sides.

3 Reclose the raw edges.

4 You have shortened one wing of your bird and created a pocket with a V-shaped opening. Leave the back wing as it is. Follow steps 1 through 6 of the Crane. Make several Cranes with one shortened wing and make one Crane in the usual manner with two full wings.

  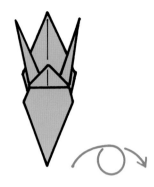

5 Fold down the full-sized wing on each bird. Then turn the models over to the side with the pocket.

 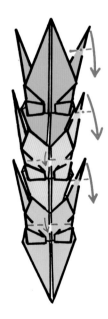

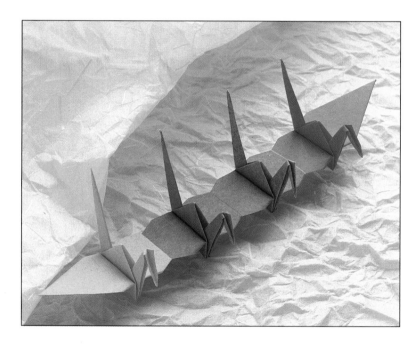

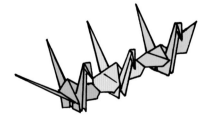

6 Join the Cranes by inserting the full-size wing of one into the pocket of another. Insert it as deeply as it will go.

7 Fold the wing with the pocket away from the body to lock the joined wings together. Inside-reverse-fold the necks to form the heads.

8 Add as many Cranes as you like to the chain. To make a lei, make a complete circle of Cranes. For extra security, you can add a drop of glue when joining the wings.

SPARROW

◆━━━━━━━━━━

Design by Gloria Farison

▲▲▲ **PAPER:** A square of almost any size or type of paper.

1 Begin with the white side (or the side that will end up as the bird's breast and feet) facing up. Diaper fold and unfold (twice): fold the square diagonally in half in both directions.

2 Rabbit Ear: put in the creases shown and then simultaneously fold both left sides to the vertical centerline. As you do so, the left corner will pinch in half and form an "ear" that sticks straight up.

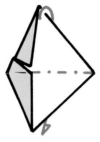

3 Mountain-fold the paper in half, bringing the top point behind to touch the bottom point.

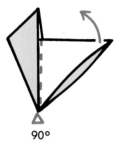

4 Lift the white triangular flap straight up.

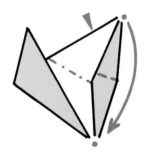

5 Squash the flap to form a small white square.

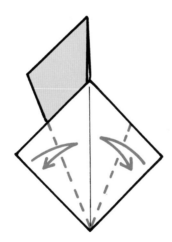

6 Ice-cream-cone fold and unfold: fold the bottom side edges of the white square to the vertical centerline. Crease and unfold.

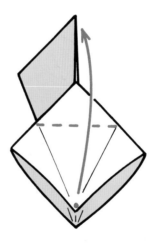

7 As you lift the front layer of the bottom corner, form a crease that connects the two creases made in the last step. The little square is opened out into a boat shape.

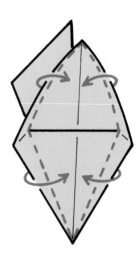

8 Bring the long raw edges together to form a tall diamond shape.

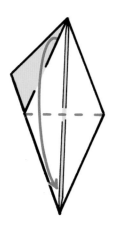 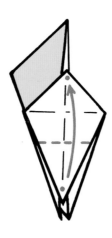  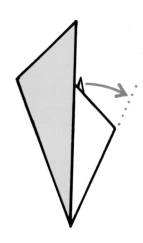

9 Fold the top point of the diamond down to the bottom to form a kite shape.

10 Fold the single bottom corner to the top of the kite.

11 Fold the left half of the kite over the right half.

12 Pull out the small tip to align with the long folded edges. (See the next drawing.)

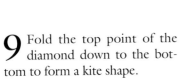 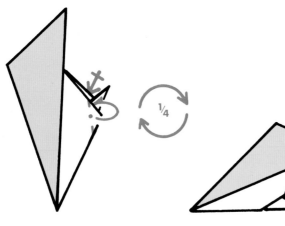  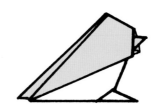

13 Mountain-fold the blunt corner of the white triangle to the interior. Repeat on the other side. Then rotate the model one quarter turn.

14 Precrease: pleat the tip back and forth with a mountain and a valley fold to form the shape of the head and beak. Unfold these creases, then open out the tip and reverse-fold it in and out on the precreases to form the bird's beak.

15 The Sparrow is complete.

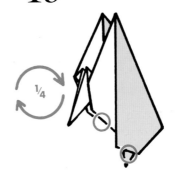

To form the Flying Pterodactyl, rotate the model so that the beak points down and becomes the tail.

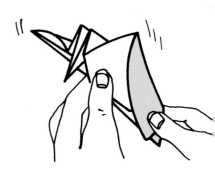

The feet of the Sparrow have become the beak of the Pterodactyl. Hold the breast (under the Pterodactyl's head) in one hand. With your other hand, pull the tail back and forth to make the wings flap.

KOALA

◆

Design by Yoshihide Momotani

▲▲▲▲ **PAPER:** A 6" (15cm) or smaller square. Origami paper or slightly heavier weight paper will work well. For a colored nose, use duo paper that is a different color on each side.

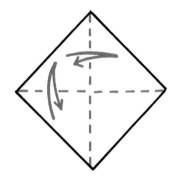

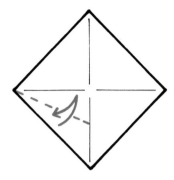

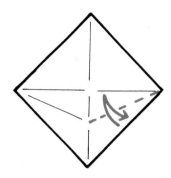

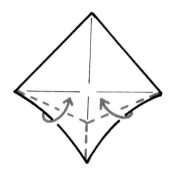

1 Diaper fold and unfold (twice): begin with the white side (or nose color) of your paper facing up. Bring one corner up to meet the opposite corner. Crease and unfold. Rotate your paper and repeat this step in the other direction.

2 Bring the bottom left edge of your paper to the horizontal centerline but crease only as far as the vertical centerline.

3 Repeat step 2 on the right side.

4 Rabbit ear: put back both creases made in steps 2 and 3 at the same time. As you do so, the bottom point will fold in half and form an "ear" that sticks up into the air.

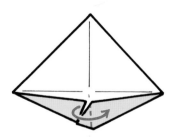

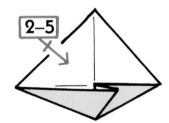

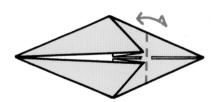

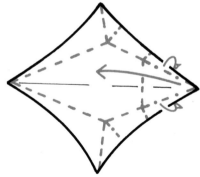

5 Fold the "ear" to the right.

6 Rabbit ear: repeat steps 2 through 5 on the top half of your paper.

7 The resulting form is known in origami as a fish base because several traditional fish models begin with this base. Make a fold where the "ears" end. Crease very sharply and unfold.

8 Open your paper and sink the right point inside the model by folding along the crease pattern shown.

71

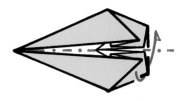

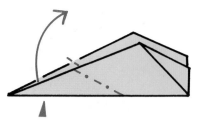

9 Mountain-fold the model in half, bringing the bottom half up and behind the top half.

10 On the long top edge, make a pinch to mark the one-half point. On the long bottom edge, make a pinch to mark the one-third point as shown in the drawing.

11 Connect the dots: make a valley fold that connects the two pinches you made in step 10. Fold and unfold.

12 Inside-reverse fold the long point along the precrease made in step 11.

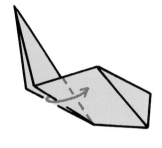

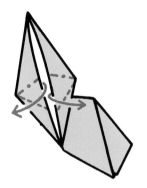

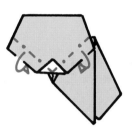

13 Open the model out to the right.

14 Following the crease pattern shown, open out the head and squash it flat into the shape shown in the next drawing.

15 Fold up a small triangle at the bottom of the head.

16 Mountain-fold the sides of the head behind as shown in the drawing.

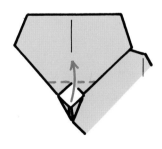

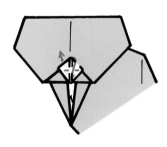

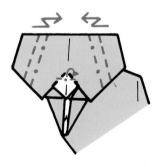

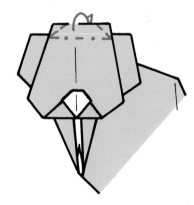

17 Detail of the head: fold up the tip of the nose.

18 Fold the tip down again, allowing the free corner to flip up at the same time.

19 Blunt the tip of the nose. Pleat the ears back and then out again.

20 Mountain-fold the top edge of the head behind, accommodating near the ears by forming little triangles. (If it is easier for you, turn the model around to the back to do this step.)

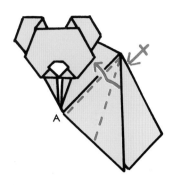

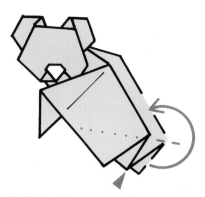

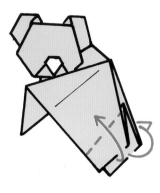

21 The loose points on the front and back will become the front legs of the Koala. Flip them up as far as they will go to create crease A. Then return them to their original position.

22 Bring the folded edge of the triangular flap to crease A, then refold on crease A. Repeat behind.

23 Inside-reverse-fold the central, hidden point at the Koala's bottom end.

24 Fold the short end up at the angle shown. Repeat behind.

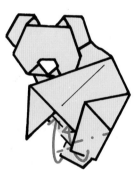

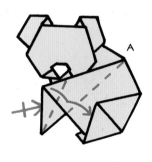

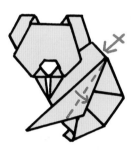

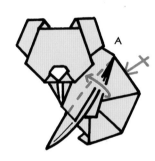

25 Mountain-fold the short edge so that it sits behind the second layer and in front of the hidden third layer. This forms the hind leg. Repeat behind.

26 Fold the front leg in half, then refold on crease A. Repeat behind.

27 Open out the paw into a long cup shape by folding on the crease shown. Repeat behind.

28 Refold the entire front leg on crease A. Repeat behind. The front legs will not lie flat because of the cup shape.

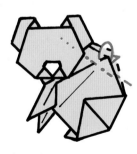

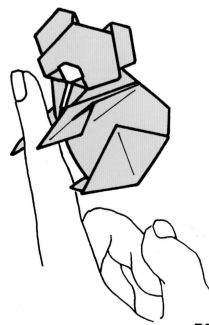

29 Mountain-fold the Koala's back inside the model. Repeat behind.

30 Your Koala is complete. The tension between the front legs will allow the Koala to clutch to your finger or a branch.

To add depth to the model, insert a finger between the layers of the Koala's back and press down on the ridge between the legs.

HOWLING DOG

◆

Design by Gay Merrill Gross

▲▲▲ **PAPER:** Make from a square, approximately 6" to 9" (15 to 23cm). This model contains several reverse folds. Be sure you are familiar with this procedure before beginning the model.

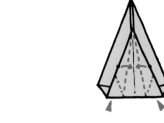

1 Begin with diamond base (see page 19). Fold bottom point up at place where obtuse corners meet on center line.

2 Smaller triangle will become tail. Narrow tail by bringing sides of this triangle to meet at center line. At same time you will need to accommodate base of triangle by squashing to make two irregularly shaped small triangles (see next drawing).

3 Lift tail and fold down at point where two bottom triangles meet.

4 Book-fold body and tail in half.

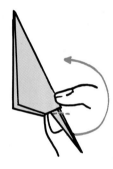

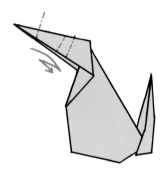

5 Outside-reverse-fold tail—slip thumb into groove of tail. As you reverse tail inside out, swing it to the side and up.

6 Outside-reverse-fold top point.

7 Outside-reverse-fold to form head.

8 To form snout: First precrease folds at end of point to desired shape (see next drawing), then unfold and form reverse folds in order shown.

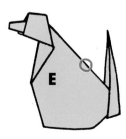
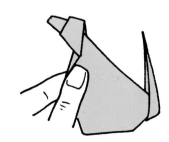

9 To make dog howl: hold dog at circle with one hand. With other hand push folded edge E (front and back) toward head end of dog.

10 Howling Dog.

Optional Nose: reverse-fold point out to front of snout. Roll up tip of point and pull up to rest at top of snout. Ear: crimp to suggest ear.

KISSING PENGUINS

◆

Design by E.D. Sullivan

▲▲▲▲ Paper: Origami paper, black on one side, white on the other. You'll need a 6" (15cm) square.

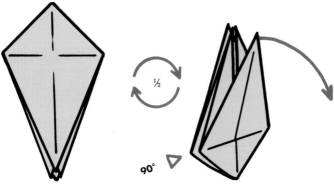

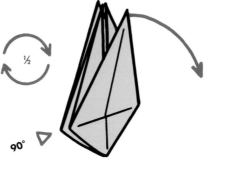

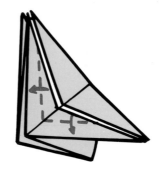

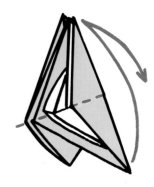

1 Begin with a black bird base. Rotate your bird base 180° so that the closed point is now at the bottom.

2 Bring top front point (wing flap) down until it stands straight out at a right angle to the rest of the model.

3 Lift one raw edge from center of model and pull away from center, exposing the white side of that layer. Crease along lines shown.

4 Reclose the wing flap to set the creases in the reverse fold you have made. When you open the wing down again, you will see that you have formed the white breast on the front of one penguin.

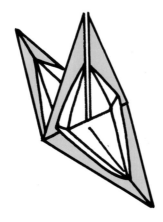

5 Repeat from step 3, on the other side and on back, trying to keep the amount that is reverse-folded out approximately equal on all sides.

6 The two points at the top of model will form the penguins' heads.

7 Outside-reverse-fold one point as shown.

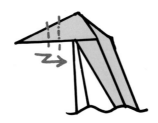

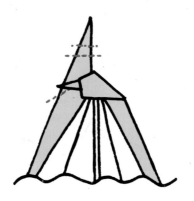

8 Reach inside head and pleat as shown to form beak.

9 Repeat steps 7 and 8 on the other point to form head and beak on that side.

10 Pull wing flaps in and out, and penguin heads will touch as if kissing. If beaks do not meet, adjust angle of heads slightly until they do.

TULIP

◆

Traditional

▲▲▲ Paper: Colorful origami paper or wrapping paper. You'll need a square approximately 4¹/₂" (12cm).

1 Begin with a waterbomb base (page 22). On front layer, fold right and left bottom points up to top point. Turn over and repeat on back of model.

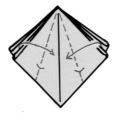

2 Turn pages: fold right-side point (front point only) over to left side. Turn over and repeat behind.

3 Beginning fold at top point, bend right and left front flaps toward each other to form a loose upside-down ice cream cone shape, but do not crease yet.

4 Slip one double-folded edge inside the other. Push together until you get a tight fit, then flatten the model so that...

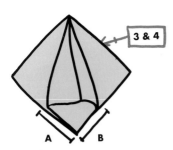

5 ...distance A equals distance B. Repeat steps 3 and 4 on back of model.

6 At bottom of model, separate front and back layers and blow into hole at bottom to inflate flower. Flatten base of flower.

7 One at a time, curl each of the four slender points at top of flower outward and "peel" down halfway to form petal.

8 Finished Tulip. Insert stem end of Standing Leaf and Stem (see page 81) into hole at bottom of flower.

STANDING LEAF AND STEM

Design by Mitsunobu Sonobe

▲ **PAPER:** Origami or any other paper in a shade of green. You'll need a square approximately 6" (15cm).

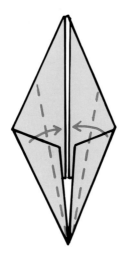

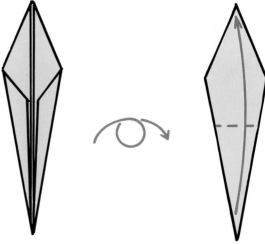

1 Begin with diamond base. Narrow bottom.

2 Turn model over from side to side (narrowed point remains at bottom).

3 Fold bottom point up to top point.

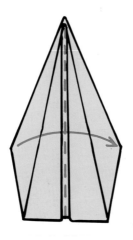

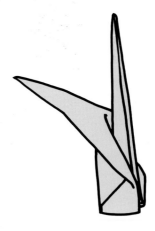

4 Book-fold in half.

5 Outside-reverse-fold outer point to form leaf. Crease softly.

6 If balanced correctly, Leaf and Stem will stand. Poke stem end into a flower with a hole at base such as the Tulip.

BUTTONHOLE FLOWER

◆

Design by Mitsunobu Sonobe

▲▲▲▲ **PAPER:** Origami paper or colored notepaper. You'll need a square 3" to 6" (7 to 15cm).

Hold model with narrow point at bottom.

View from side.

1 Follow instructions for the umbrella base through step 10, reversing all color instructions so that the inside of the model will be colored. When the flower is opened, the color will show. Precrease: make diagonal valley folds starting at colored point. (You are folding through all layers of paper.) Then pinch narrow point in half with a mountain fold.

2 At the top of the flower you have eight flaps, which will become petals. Pull the two outermost flaps toward each other until they meet and the rest of the petals spread apart as flower opens.

3 Insert thumb into one petal, and give it a round shape by flattening the outer slanted folded edge between thumb and index finger. To set this shape and keep petal open, push up slightly with forefinger, creating a small mountain crease. Repeat on all petals.

4 Buttonhole Flower in full bloom. Insert stem end into the pocket of the Buttonhole Leaf and Stem or the Cactus Plant (see pages 83 and 84).

BUTTONHOLE LEAF AND STEM

Variation on design by Alice Gray

▲ **PAPER:** Origami paper or similar paper in a shade of green. Use the same size square you used to fold the Buttonhole Flower.

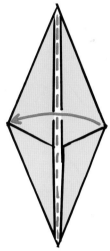

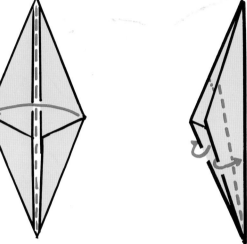

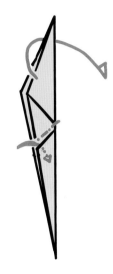

1 Begin with a diamond base (page 19). Hold it so that the sides folded to center last are at the bottom of model. Wide V formed by folded edges points to stem end. Book-fold model in half.

2 Narrow stem end of front layer. Turn over and repeat behind.

3 Find lower pocket and mountain-fold leaf end back, creating a crease that is slightly above and parallel to the folded edge of pocket.

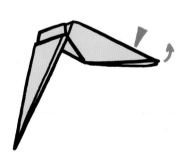

4 To shape leaf, push down at mountain fold near end of leaf, slightly curling up tip of leaf.

5 Insert stem end of flower into pocket.

6 Mountain-pinch pocket area in half. This will narrow stem and help to hold flower securely. For added security, place glue on stem end of flower before inserting into pocket in step 5.

CACTUS PLANT

◆

Variation on designs by Mitsunobu Sonobe, Rae Cooker, and Florence Temko

▲▲▲ **PAPER:** Origami or wrapping paper in a shade of green. You'll need a square approximately 6" to 8" (15 to 20cm).

Fold Teardrop Ornament (see page 90) up to step 5.

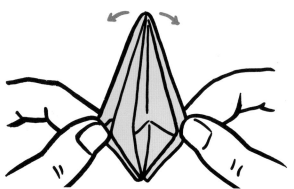

1 Separate all eight side flaps so that they are equidistant from one another.

2 Hold two opposite flaps between thumb and forefinger of each hand. As you slowly pull your hands apart, the top point will begin to spread apart and flatten. As soon as the tip is slightly flattened, move your hands to hold two different opposite flaps and spread the tip out a little further. Continue rotating the flaps you tug at as you spread the top of the model until it loses its point and is rounded to your liking.

3 Finished cactus. Insert tiny Buttonhole Flower (see page 82) into one pocket of plant and let the cactus rest on a Flowerpot (see page 49).

◆ Decorations and Accessories

SECRET RING

Design by Ranana Benjamin

▲▲ **PAPER:** You'll need a rectangular strip approximately 1¼" wide × 6¼" long (3.5×16cm). For a larger ring, start with a longer strip.

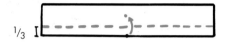

1 Begin with the white side facing up. Fold long bottom edge up ⅓.

2 Fold top edge down to bottom folded edge, along the raw edge you just folded up.

3 Rotate strip 90° so long edges are at sides. Scale of next drawing is larger and shows only top end of strip.

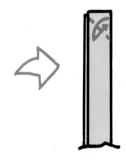

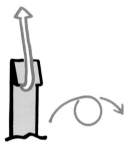

4 Bring top short edge to lie over long edge, make a diagonal crease, and unfold.

5 Using the bottom of your diagonal crease as a guide, fold top short edge down to form a tab that lies directly over rest of strip.

6 Fold down along raw edges.

7 Unfold both horizontal creases, then turn strip over.

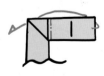

8 Swing top of strip diagonally to right so that lower horizontal crease lines up with right long edge.

9 Fold down along horizontal folded edge.

10 Mountain-fold short horizontal strip behind longer vertical strip and swing around to left.

11 Notice the pocket created by the diagonal fold at the top of the long strip. Fold over the short tab sticking out at the left and tuck into pocket.

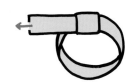

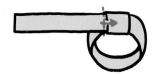

12 Bend top ("stone") end and bottom end toward each other, forming a loop.

13 Insert bottom end under top layer of stone. Slide through until it comes out the other side of the stone.

14 Pull loose end to adjust size of Ring. Try on your finger to test.

15 When Ring band fits your finger, set the size by folding the loose strip over the stone.

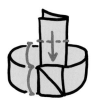

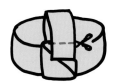

16 Fold strip diagonally down so top edge lies over folded edge at left.

17 Bend strip back and slip up through Ring. Crease strip at bottom edge of Ring band.

18 Fold end of strip down so that height of strip will equal height of stone.

Note: if you made the size of your Ring band very small, part of the overhang you folded down in step 18 may lie over stone. If this is the case, cut off the part that lies over stone.

19 Fold strip down over stone, then tuck into triangular pocket.

20 Finished Ring.

For Secret Ring: slip tab back out of triangular pocket. Insert a tiny photo or secret message and tuck tab back into pocket. The tab will keep your secret hidden.

Diamond Ring

◆

Design by Ranana Benjamin

▲▲▲ **PAPER:** Foil paper. You'll need a rectangular strip approximately 1¼" wide x 6¼" long (3.5 x 16cm). For a larger ring, start with a longer strip.

  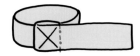

Fold Secret Ring up to step 15.

1 Fold strip diagonally down so that top edge lies over folded edge at left. Unfold.

2 Repeat last step, this time bringing bottom edge of strip diagonally up to lie on left folded edge. Unfold.

3 The two creases you just made form an X at left end of your strip. Mountain-fold strip back at right end of X. Crease and unfold.

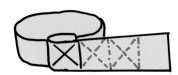 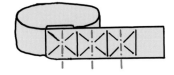 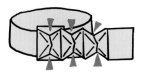 

4 You now have an X enclosed in a square at left side of your strip. Repeat steps 1 through 3 two more times, creating two more X patterns in squares on your strip.

5 Put a vertical mountain fold through center of each X. After each crease is made, unfold and make next crease.

　Check your model. All diagonal creases should be valley folds, all vertical creases should be mountain folds.

6 Starting at first X, push in at vertical mountain fold that divides X in half. Using existing creases, collapse small square that outlines X into a half-closed waterbomb base form. Repeat on next two X patterns.

7 Tuck tab at end of strip into pocket on Ring band. (If tab is too long and extends out other end, you can cut off a little to shorten tab before inserting.)

8 Finished Ring.

Side View.

Teardrop Ornament

Design by Rae Cooker

▲▲▲ **PAPER:** Origami paper, foil paper, wrapping paper, or decorated handmade Japanese papers. For the ornament, you'll need a 4" to 6" (10–15cm) square. For earrings, you'll need approximately 2" (5cm) square.

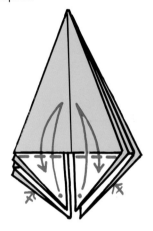 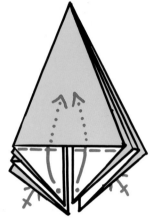 

> **Follow the instructions for the umbrella base through step 6 to get to a squashed preliminary base.**

1 Below the tall triangle are four small triangle "feet"— two in front and two in back. Lift both front triangle feet as far up as they will go. Unfold. Turn over and repeat behind.

2 Hold model loosely. Using the creases you just made, tuck each small triangle underneath raw edge of tall triangle. Repeat behind.

The side flaps will now be locked together in pairs at the base of your model. You will have four double flaps — two double flaps on the right and two double flaps on the left.

3 Begin to lift up one double flap as if you were turning the page of a book, but stop when the flap is standing straight up, at a right angle to the rest of the model.

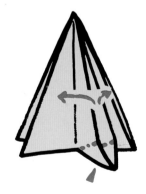 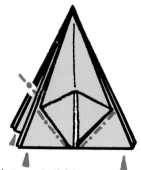 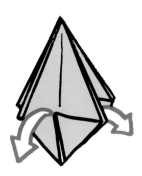 

4 Insert finger between the double layers. At the same time push up at the bottom edge where the layers are locked together until entire flap squashes flat.

5 Squash fold: repeat steps 3 and 4 on remaining three double flaps.

6 Insert finger into pocket formed by squash fold and open out slightly. Repeat on other three pockets.

7 Finished Teardrop Ornament. Hang from a thread or wire.

CHINESE LUCKY STAR

◆

Traditional Design

▲▲ **PAPER:** A narrow strip approximately 1/2" x 10" (1.3 x 25cm) or of similar proportions. Foil paper will work well. (See page 85 for photograph of Lucky Stars.)

  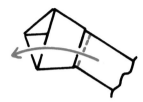 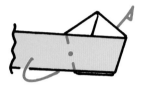

1 With the white side facing up, loosely tie the strip into a knot at the left end. The shape of the knot should form an even pentagon. Adjust the long and short tails accordingly.

2 Fold the short tail of the pentagon-shaped knot. The short tail should not extend beyond the pentagon. If it does, snip or fold it a little shorter.

3 Fold the long tail over the short raw edge at one side of the pentagon and toward an opposite edge. Since a pentagon has an odd number of sides, an opposite side could be one of two sides. If you begin with a very even pentagon, the tail should naturally lean toward one of these two sides, and that will be your guide to tell you which direction to wind the tail.

4 Wrap the tail around the knot and toward an opposite side.

 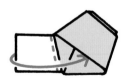 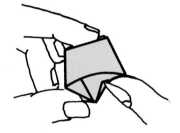

5 Continue wrapping the long tail around the pentagon in a manner that retains the even pentagon shape. As you wind the tail, make soft, not hard, creases to give the shape a slight puffiness.

6 Tuck the very end of the tail under the raw edge to lock it in place. If the tail is a little too long to do this, snip a little off and then tuck it under.

7 You should now have a multi-layered, even pentagon-shaped "button." It is important that the shape be a little puffy and not completely flat. Hold the button between two fingers at the side edges. Do not hold the top and bottom surfaces. With your other hand, push in gently with your thumbnail at the center of one edge, causing it to indent inward. Repeat this step on all five sides to form a puffy star shape.

8 The finished Lucky Star.

A GARLAND OF STARS:

Before you being winding the tail around the pentagonal knot (step 3), lay a thin cord or thread over the knot and then proceed to wind the tail, enclosing the cord inside the star. Alternatively, you can use needle and thread to string finished stars together.

FIVE-DIAMOND DECORATION

Design by Mike Thomas

▲▲ **PAPER:** A rectangle in the proportions 1:7. (To make a Three-Diamond Decoration use a 1:4 rectangle.) If you start with a slightly longer rectangle, you can cut off the excess when the model is complete. This will prevent you from running short of paper if your folding is not perfectly accurate.

> **This model can also be made from a US dollar bill or other currency of similar size. Fold the bill lengthwise into thirds and then begin from step 1.**

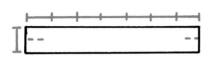

1 Begin with the white side facing up. Pinch the midpoint of each short side.

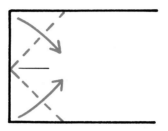

2 Fold the top and bottom left corners to the horizontal centerline.

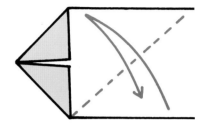

3 Fold the long bottom edge up to lie along the edges of the two small triangles. Crease and unfold.

4 Repeat step 3, folding the top edge down and then unfolding.

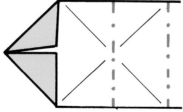

5 You should now see an X on your strip made up of two valley folds. Add a mountain fold at the vertical center of the X and at the right side of the X.

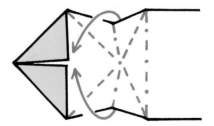

6 Push in on the mountain and valley folds of the X and form them into the shape of a waterbomb base, collapsing it to the left.

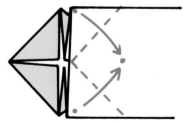

7 Fold the two new corners down to the horizontal centerline.

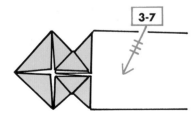

8 Repeat steps 3 through 7 three more times until your paper appears as in the next drawing.

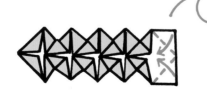

9 Fold the top and bottom right corners to the horizontal centerline. Then turn your model over.

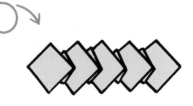

10 The Five-Diamond Decoration is finished.

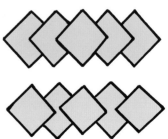

VARIATIONS:
By rearranging the folds, the diamonds can be formed into different patterns.

HEART LOCKET

◆

Design by Gay Merrill Gross

▲▲▲ **PAPER:** Foil paper, origami paper, or gift wrap approximately 6" (15cm) square. Skilled folders can make a heart from smaller-size squares.

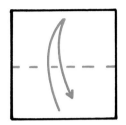 

1 Book fold and unfold: with the white side facing up, fold the square in half and unfold. Rotate the paper one quarter turn so that the center crease is now vertical.

2 Make a large pinch at the center of the vertical crease.

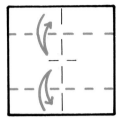

3 Cupboard fold and unfold: bring the bottom and top edges inward to meet at the center pinch mark. Crease and unfold.

4 Match the dots: bring the bottom edge up to the farthest crease, make a small pinch at the middle of the folded edge and unfold.

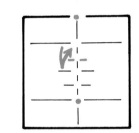 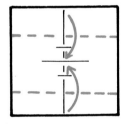

5 Match the dots: bring the top edge down to the farthest crease, make a small pinch at the middle of the folded edge, and unfold.

6 Cupboard-fold on the existing creases.

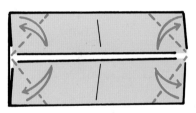

7 Fold each outside corner to the horizontal centerline. Crease sharply and unfold.

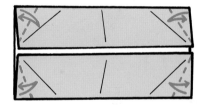

8 Fold in each corner so that the double raw edge lies on the nearest crease. Crease sharply and unfold.

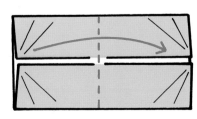

9 Book fold: bring the left side over to the right side, folding the paper in half. Then rotate the paper one quarter turn so that the folded edge is at the top.

10 Using the two small pinch marks on the folded edge as a guide, fold the two top corners down to form two small triangles as shown in the next drawing.

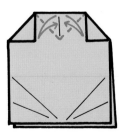

11 Fold each half of the small top edge to lie along the vertical edge of the nearest small triangle. Make each fold separately; crease sharply and unfold.

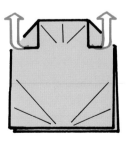

12 Unfold the two small triangles.

13 Fold each top corner so that the double-folded edge at the side lies along the nearest crease.

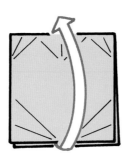

14 Unfold the top folded edge.

15 Change the four small creases shown to valley creases.

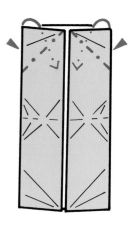

16 Inside reverse fold: slightly separate the front and back layers of paper and push the top corners in between these two layers, folding on the existing creases.

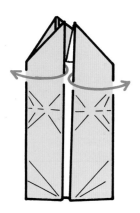

17 Separate the raw edges that meet in the center, slightly opening the "doors."

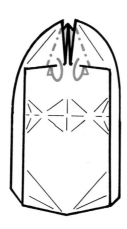

18 Narrow the interior triangular flaps by mountain-folding the edge of the flaps behind. You are folding on existing creases. Then reclose the "doors."

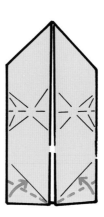

19 Fold up on the existing creases.

20 Fold the model in half from top to bottom.

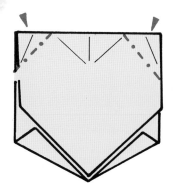

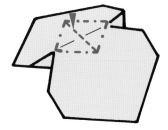

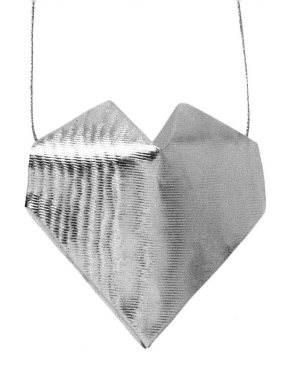

21 Inside reverse fold: push the top corners between the front and back layers, folding on the existing creases.

22 View from top of model: separate the front and back layers, then push down at the center of the top-folded edge. A diamond-shaped indentation should pop downward.

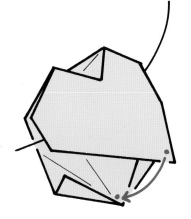

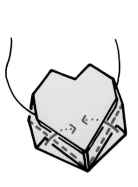

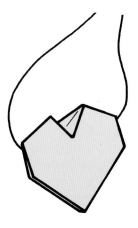

23 (Cutaway view.) Reach inside the model and narrow the two small triangular flaps by mountain-folding on the existing creases.

24 Insert a small photo, message, or object between the layers of the heart. Lay a decorative cord across the opening. Press the bottom points together to hold the heart closed.

25 Insert the side flaps of the back layer into the pockets of the top layer.

26 Completed Heart Locket.

HEXAHEDRON

◆

Design by Molly Kahn

▲▲ **PAPER:** Three squares of equal size.

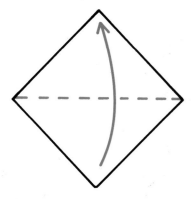

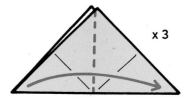

1 Begin with the white side facing up. Diaper fold: fold the bottom corner up to the top corner.

2 Fold the side points up to the top of the triangle. Crease sharply and unfold.

3 Fold the triangle in half, making a sharp crease. Repeat steps 1 through 3 on all three units.

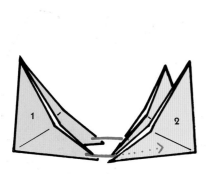

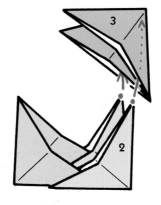

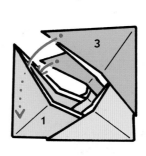

4 Hold unit one so that the arms (two loose points) are at the bottom and point right. Hold unit two so the arms are at the right and point up. Insert the arms of unit one into the pockets (double layer on either side of the center crease) on unit two.

5 Hold unit three so that the arms are at the top and point left. Insert the arms of unit two into the pockets of unit three.

6 As you insert the arms of unit three into the pockets of unit one, open out the model so that it takes a three-dimensional shape.

7 Slide all three units together as far as possible and your Hexahedron is complete.

To hang, insert a thread or wire before completely sliding all the units together. The model can be hung from either a wide point or a narrow point.

IDEAS FOR USING HEXAHEDRON

These ideas came from John Blackman, who specializes in creating practical uses for the origami models he folds.

Ornament: hang the Hexahedron singly or hang several in graduated sizes.

Gift Box: a small gift, such as a piece of jewelry, can be enclosed inside the Hexahedron. For a see-through container, fold the units from sheets of plastic such as those used for report covers.

Pomander: fill the Hexahedron with potpourri or spray cologne on a piece of cotton and enclose it in the model. Hang the pomander from a decorative cord.

Earrings: make a pair of small Hexahedrons and hang them from thread or wire attached to an earring clip.

Necklace: as you string several hexahedrons on a decorative cord, knot the cord before and after each "bead" to hold it in place.

Fortune Cookie: write some humorous fortunes on little slips of paper and enclose each inside a Hexahedron. Add a small party favor if you wish.

JOINED HEXAHEDRONS

Half-a-Ball: four Hexahedrons (twelve units) can be glued together to form a decorative shape with a flat bottom.

Magnet Decoration: attach a magnet with a self-adhesive backing (sold at craft supply stores) to the flat surface of the model. The model can now be used to hold notes and messages on metal surfaces such as refrigerator doors or file cabinets.

Decorative Ball: eight hexahedrons (twenty-four units) can be glued together to form a ball taking the shape of a stellated octahedron. First form two Half-a-Ball models. Glue the two halves together, back to back.

Hanging Ball: before gluing the two Half-a-Ball models together, sandwich a wire loop or a loop of decorative cord in between the two halves.

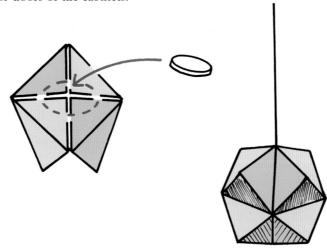

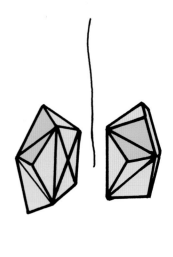

FLUTED DIAMOND

◆

Design by Molly Kahn

▲▲▲ **PAPER**: Two squares of equal size.

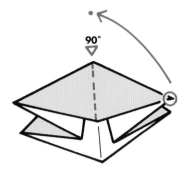

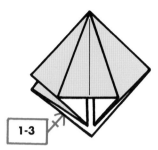

1 Begin with preliminary base (page 20) positioned so that the closed corner is away from you. Lift one flap from the right and swing it upward until it stands at a right angle to the rest of the paper.

2 Squash fold: press down on the folded edge of the flap, causing the raw edges to spread apart.

3 Flatten the flap into a tall triangular shape. Make sure the centerline of the tall triangle lies dead center by aligning it with the gap between the two small triangular "feet" below it. Turn your paper over and repeat steps 1 through 3 on the back.

4 Turn the page: flip the right half of the tall triangular shape over to the left. Turn the paper over and repeat behind.

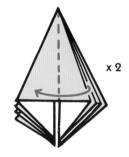

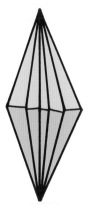

5 On the right you have exposed one of the full-size flaps from your original preliminary base. Repeat steps 1 through 3 on this flap, then turn the model over and repeat behind.

6 You have now squashed all four flaps of your original preliminary base. This completes one unit of your model. With your second square, make another unit, exactly the same as the first.

7 Looking at the top, closed end of each unit, spread the flaps away from each other, until all eight flaps are the same distance from each other.

9 Slide the two units together as far as possible and arrange the flaps so that they are evenly spaced.

If you are going to hang this model as an ornament, you may wish to insert the thread, cord, or wire before joining the two units.

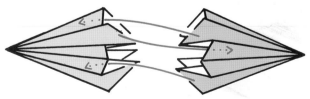

8 To join the two units: turn the units sideways and hold them so that the open ends face each other. Notice that the surface between two flaps either ends with a point (we will consider this a tab) or a raw edge (we will consider this a pocket). The tabs on one unit will be inserted into the pockets of the second unit and vice versa. This is a little tricky, but not too difficult if you have a little patience.

HANGING ORNAMENTS

Many origami designs can be used to make decorative ornaments. Here are some basic techniques for hanging an origami model.

NEEDLE AND THREAD

SINGLE MODELS

Put a needle and thread though the model and tie a small knot to hold the thread in place.

MULTIPLE MODELS

Use a long needle and strong thread and insert them through the entire model. Continue stringing the models on the same thread. Use a small button or bead, a small ornamental model, or a large knot at the beginning of the chain to prevent the models from slipping off.

WIRE LOOP

Bend a thin wire around a round stick or skewer to form a loop. Twist the two "tails" tightly together for approximately 1" (2.5cm). Cut off the excess wire. Slip the wire loop off the stick. Glue the twisted end of the wire into a hole poked in the model.

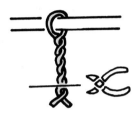

Thread a ribbon, cord, or thread through the loop and hang the model.

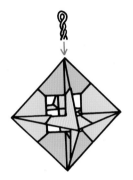

CORD

Fancy cords can add a decorative touch to your ornament. Try metallic cord, tassel cord, or thin ribbon. Thread or nylon fishing line will make your model appear to "float" in midair. A model hanging from thin elastic cord can add a bouncing effect. It is usually preferable to attach the cord before the model is complete.

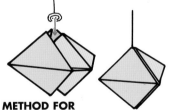

METHOD FOR HANGING MODULARS

1 Attach a "button" to the end of your cord. The "button" can be an actual small button, a sequin, a bead, a piece of crumpled aluminum foil, a small piece of a drinking straw, or a small scrap of paper.

2 Slightly separate some of the units on your modular and drop the "button" inside. Reclose the modular and hang the model from the cord.

POKED HOLE METHOD:

1 Fold the model up to the base it is made from (or unfold it to this stage). Spread the base out to half-open position and poke a hole through the center point of the paper with a pin or needle.

2 Also poke a hole through a tiny scrap of medium-weight paper.

3 Bend a very thin wire in half.

4 Tie the two ends of your cord together and slip the cord between the points of the wire.

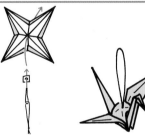

5 Insert the wire through the hole in the paper scrap and pull the scrap down to the knot end of the cord.

6 Insert the wire through the inside of the base and pull the cord out the top of the base.

7 Slip the wire off the cord and complete the folding of the model.

JEWELRY

Origami models can be turned into unique, wearable jewelry. Customize your jewelry by choosing papers that match your wardrobe or your color scheme. Besides the origami models, you will need jewelry findings (such as earring wires, earring clips, pin backs, and barrette clips). These can be purchased in a craft or jewelry supply store. Depending on the model, you may want to give it a protective coating.

PINS AND BARRETTES

Attach a flat origami model to the pin back or barrette clip using a strong adhesive such as a glue, craft or jewelry cement, or five-minute epoxy.

EARRINGS

Attach an eye pin or head pin (available at craft or jewelry supply stores) to your model by gluing it onto or inserting it through the model and bending a small loop at the end with round-nose pliers. If the pin is too long, it can be cut with wire cutters. Beads can also be added. Hook the loop at the end of the pin onto the earring wire or clip.

If you do not have eye pins or head pins, you can make a loop for hanging the model to the clasp by using strong thread and a needle or a very thin wire looped around a toothpick and twisted.

PROTECTIVE COATINGS

(see page 114 for more information)

Clear Acrylic Spray: spray the model outdoors or in a very well ventilated area. Several coats may be needed.

Nail Polish: paint on clear nail polish. For a sparkle effect, use clear nail polish that comes with glitter in the bottle.

Acrylic Medium and **Varnish:** such products come in gloss or matte finishes. Apply the varnish with a dampened brush. Several coats may be needed.

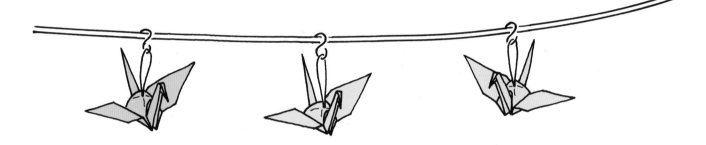

ORIGAMI FOR PARTIES

The colorful and playful shapes of origami make them a wonderful way to add a festive touch to a party. Here are ideas for using some of the models in this book.

INVITATIONS

Write your message directly on a flat origami model or attach the model to a card.

DECORATIONS

Prepare origami models as hanging ornaments by attaching a decorative cord. Drape a ribbon or cord across the room. Hang the origami ornaments from the ribbon using wire hooks, an unbent paper clip, or thread. As guests leave, remove an ornament and present it to each of them as a gift.

For a very dramatic effect, hang a large flock of Cranes individually from long ribbon or thread in varying lengths. Attach each ribbon to the ceiling or other high structure. In Hawaii, a thousand Cranes hung in this manner are sometimes seen at celebratory occasions such as weddings and anniversaries.

CANDY CUPS

Make a basket by gluing a paper or ribbon handle to an origami box. Fill the basket with nuts, candy, or other snacks.

HORS D'OEUVRE PICKS

Fold tiny origami models and glue them to the top of toothpicks.

PLACE CARDS

Write each guest's name on a card and use the Card Holder model to stand the cards up at each place setting. If you are giving a dinner party, the Card Holder can be used to display the evening's menu.

PARTY FAVORS

Many of the action toys make delightful party favors to give away.

CORSAGE

Corsage arrangement by Pearl Chin, based on a traditional design

▲▲▲ **PAPER**: For the best result, use paper that is colored on both sides. You will need one 6" (5cm) square for the leaf and several small squares (appro mately 2" [15cm[to a side) for the flowers. For the flower centers, you will need some small paper strips (colored on both sides) approximately 3/16" x 3/ (0.4 x 2cm).

MATERIALS

To assemble the corsage, you will need thin florist wire and florist tape (both are available at craft stores or florist supply shops). Alternatively, you can use any thin wire and crepe-paper strips that can be wound around the wire with a little glue. You will need a wire cutter and needle-nose pliers. If these are not available, try a pair of strong scissors and strong tweezers.

FLOWER

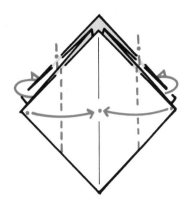

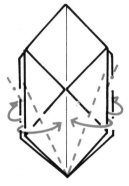

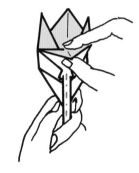

1 Begin with a preliminary base (see page 20) positioned as shown. If your paper is colored on only one side, reverse the color instructions for the preliminary base to give you a white base with a colored inside. Fold the side corners of the front layer to the center. Turn the paper over and repeat behind.

2 The open end of the paper should be away from you. Narrow the closed end by folding the lower edges of the front layer to the center. Turn the paper over and repeat behind.

3 Hold the stem end, then open the flower by pulling down on one of the top points. The flower should "blossom" open, showing four petals. Then pinch the stem end in half with a small mountain fold.

FLOWER WIRING

4 Your flower is complete and ready to be wired. If you wish, curl the tips of the petals with your fingers to curve them up or down.

1 With a wire cutter, cut a 6" (15cm) length of thin florist wire for each flower. With needle-nose pliers, form a small loop at one end of the wire and insert one of the small strips. When the strip is centered, close the loop by pressing it between the broad end of the pliers.

2 Insert the bottom end of the wire into the flower and poke a hole through the bottom tip of the flower. Pull the wire down until a little of the flower center (the strip) sticks out between the petals.

3 Cut a short piece of florist tape from the roll (approximately 5" [13cm] long) and stretch it slightly. (Stretching the florist tape releases the wax that enables the florist tape to stick to itself.) Begining at the stem end of the flower, wrap the tape a few times around the base of the flower. This is done by holding the tape taut and slightly stretching it with one hand as you slowly twist the flower with your other hand.

4 After the stem end of the flower is covered with tape, slant the tape at a downward angle and continue twirling the wire as you hold the tape taut. Ideally, you want to pull the tape as tautly as you can without tearing it. Continue twisting the wire until the entire stem is covered. If there is any excess tape at the bottom, cut it off and pinch the bottom of the stem so that any loose tail of tape will stick to the rest of the tape.

When all of your flowers have centers and stems you are ready to assemble the corsage.

ASSEMBLY:

1 Place the large leaf square on the table so that one corner points toward you. Arrange the flowers on the leaf in a staggered fashion. When you are satisfied with the arrangement, pick up the wires of all the flowers at once, trying not to disturb the arrangement.

2 Approximately 1" (2.5cm) below the lowest flower, begin wrapping all of the stems together with a short piece of florist tape. Continue wrapping for a couple of inches, until all of the flowers are held together securely.

3 Now gather the bottom corner of the leaf square around the flower stems. When you are satisfied with the position of the leaf, begin wrapping another piece of florist tape around the base of the leaf, attaching it to the flower stems. Continue wrapping the tape at a slanted angle until you have tightly wrapped all of the stems together and reached the bottom of the lowest stem.

4 Tie a ribbon into a bow at the base of the leaf and bend the end of the stems backward to hide it behind the flowers. Use a long straight pin to wear your corsage, or use it as a decoration.

◆ *Part III*
PAPERS and SPECIAL TECHNIQUES

PAPERS

WASHI PAPER

Washi paper is a very high-quality paper made in Japan. Unlike most commercially available paper, it is not produced in huge quantities by machines, but is handmade in Japan using special techniques and materials. Some papers are left in a neutral color or given a solid color, but much washi paper is also made with exquisite designs and patterns, some so elegant that they almost appear to be brocaded fabric. Because of the paper's softness, origami models made with washi will give a different effect than those made with other papers. Washi paper is not as readily available as other kinds of paper and can be quite expensive, especially for the more decorative patterns. Nevertheless, washi paper will add a lot to the strength and beauty of the finished model.

PACKAGED ORIGAMI PAPER

The most common packaged origami paper you will find has a solid color on one side and is white on the reverse side. Most packages contain a rainbow of colors; occasionally you may find packages containing only one color. While these packaged papers commonly come in 6" (15cm) squares, you can usually also find 3" (7.5cm), $4\frac{1}{2}$" (12cm), and 10" (25cm) squares. As the popularity of origami has grown, so has the variety of packaged papers made for folding. Such paper is now available in an exciting assortment of patterns, designs, and textures.

FOIL PAPER

Foil paper is not the aluminum foil used in the kitchen. Such foil is too thin to fold successfully unless you bond it first to another paper (see page 112). Foil paper suitable for origami is manufactured with a layer of foil bonded to a layer of paper. The foil side may be smooth or have an embossed pattern. It is readily available in rolls along with other gift wraps, especially in gold, silver, green, and red at Christmas time. It is also available for sale as precut squares along with other packaged origami papers.

    The brilliant, shiny surface of foil paper can be very attractive for certain models, while others may look better with a more subdued surface. Foil offers the advantage of allowing you to shape and mold the paper. One disadvantage, however, is that crease lines are usually more obvious on foil paper, so if your model requires a lot of precreasing, you may end up with several unwanted crease lines showing on the finished model.

WRAPPING PAPER

Most wrapping papers are ideal for origami. Choose a weight and pattern suitable for the model you are making. Paper used by florists to wrap flowers can also be suitable for origami. One type of paper to avoid, however, is heavyweight, highly glossed wrapping paper. This paper tends to crack along a crease line and creases do not stay well, so a finished model will tend to unfold.

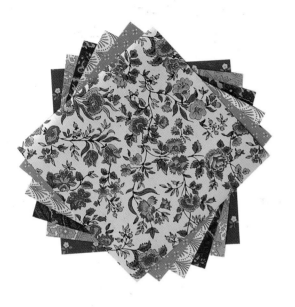

WALLPAPER

The key word here is paper. Many wall coverings today are made from vinyl, which will not fold well. If "all-paper" wallpaper cannot be found, look for wallpaper that has a paper backing. Among the wallpapers made from paper, some may crack excessively when folded, but others will fold well, and when used for an appropriate model can yield some spectacular results.

FREE PAPER

One of the appeals of origami is its low cost and the minimal amount of materials required. Indeed, there are many excellent sources of papers that cost absolutely nothing. Just bear in mind that different weights and types of paper should be matched to the appropriate kind of model. (Most origami models require a lightweight paper.) Here is a list of some "free" sources of paper; keep your eyes open and you will probably discover others.

- discarded flyers
- used envelopes from greeting cards
- foil linings from envelopes
- business envelopes with an interesting pattern on the inside
- leftover wallpaper
- leftover gift wrap
- sample books of wallpaper

- leftover florist paper
- paper bags
- decorative shopping bags
- old magazine covers
- decorative photos or drawings from last year's calendar
- old music sheets
- computer paper
- stationery
- maps

TECHNIQUES EXPLAINED

PAPER PAINTING

MATERIALS:

- old newspaper to protect work surface
- sponges
- liquid watercolors (come in dropper bottles, available at art-supply stores)
- cup of water
- paper sturdy enough to withstand slight dampening (suggested: paper side of foil-backed paper, kraft paper, paper bag, stationery, onion skin paper)
- wooden spring clothespins (optional)

(Note: besides liquid watercolors, you can experiment with other types of paint, such as acrylic paint thinned with water, for example)

1 Cover table or other work surface with several layers of newspaper or other protective covering.
2 Place over newspaper the paper you wish to paint.
3 Cut sponge into smaller pieces. Simple rectangles (approximately 2" x 1½" is a convenient size) will work or you can cut the sponge into patterns or shapes. A pattern or waffling on the surface of your sponge can be useful in creating interesting patterns on your paper.
4 Dampen sponge by dipping it in water, then squeeze all the water out.
5 Clamp the clothespin to one end of the sponge. (If you don't mind getting watercolor on your hands, you can hold the sponge directly.)
6 Pick a color and drop a few drops on the end of the sponge.
7 Using the clothespin as a handle, dab the paper with the end of the sponge on which you put color. If too much color comes out of the sponge, dab it onto a piece of scrap paper first until the dye comes out in an amount that will color your paper without soaking it.

Experiment with these different methods of painting your paper:

- After you have added one color to your paper, change sponges and add another color.
- To lighten the color or create a bleeding effect with colors running into one another, slightly dampen your paper with a moist sponge before adding color.
- If you want your paper to be a solid color, slide your sponge across the paper in long strokes instead of dabbing. Use horizontal and then vertical strokes to avoid a streaked look. If the sponge does not go across paper easily, you may want to dampen the paper a little first.
- Instead of using a different sponge for each color, you can achieve another interesting effect by dropping two or three colors on the end of one sponge. Try to separate the colors slightly or they will end up blending, and instead of two or three separate colors you will have an new color. You can now create multicolored swirls, stripes, or spots with one touch of your sponge.
- You may want to give your paper a background color. If so, let it dry, and then add a pattern.

- Experiment with other ways of transferring the color onto the paper, such as placing the color on a piece of string and dragging it over or dabbing it on the paper.

DUO PAPER

In some origami models, both sides of the paper may show on the finished model. If your paper is white on the reverse side and you prefer the effect of two contrasting colors or a color and a pattern, you may be able to find wrapping paper or special origami paper, called duo paper, that has a different color on each side. In addition, you can achieve some very dramatic results by trying one of these methods:

- Use the paper-painting techniques on this page to give a color or pattern to one side of your paper.
- Start with, or cut, two sheets into squares of the same size. Place the sheets together, with their back or white sides facing each other. Treat this double layer of paper as one sheet and fold the model as usual.
- Use a spray adhesive such as Spray Mount™ (available in art-supply stores) to join your two sheets together before folding. When using a spray adhesive, be sure you are in a well-ventilated space, or outdoors. Protect the area where you will be working with lots of old newspaper. Place the smaller of the two papers you wish to bond together on top of newspaper with the back side up. Spray the sheet with adhesive. Carefully lift this sheet and lay it over the second sheet, back sides touching. Press flat. Use a scissors or paper cutter to cut the bonded papers to the size and shape you need for your model.
- Remember that it is always the back side of each sheet that is bonded to the other.

COPIER–DESIGNED PAPERS

You can use a photocopying machine to create interesting patterns on paper. Look through books, advertisements, wrapping papers, and decorated bags for geometrics and other patterns to photocopy, then use one of the following methods to copy the pattern onto white or colored photocopier paper:

- Copy the design as is.
- Enlarge or reduce the design.
- Move paper on the glass as the photocopier is operating
- to give a swirling effect.
- Experiment with photocopying textured surfaces such as a crumpled sheet of aluminum foil.

WET FOLDING

Some heavy papers that are not ordinarily ideal for folding are excellent candidates for wet folding. The water softens the paper so it does not crack when folded, and because of the stiffness of the paper, your model, when dry, will be much sturdier than if folded from softer paper. A wet-folded model also offers the folder the option of shaping a model such as an animal into a more three-dimensional form, giving it a more sculptured, life-like appearance.

The technique of wet folding was pioneered by the Japanese origami master, Akira Yoshizawa.

TECHNIQUE:

The main idea is to keep the paper slightly damp while you are folding. If you are using paper that will crack if not wet, dampen it before doing any folding. If you are using stiff paper that you want to be able to mold later, it is preferable to do some of the beginning folds first (such as preliminary or waterbomb base), and then begin dampening the paper.

Fill a shallow bowl with some water. Dampen a sponge or washcloth in the water and use it to gently moisten your paper. Be careful not to wet the paper too much, especially at points on the paper where you will have a lot of intersecting creases. An example is the very center of the paper, which will tend to weaken from the many creases there and will tear if too wet.

As you continue folding, the paper will have a tendency to dry. Keep using your sponge or washcloth to dampen areas you are working on that have dried.

When the model is completely folded you can begin to mold and shape the paper to give the animal more form. If the paper is not damp enough to allow shaping, use your sponge to dampen it, or at this point you can spray your model lightly with a spray bottle or water mister. If necessary, paper towels can be used to stuff inside the model. Specific positions of joints or other features can be held in place until the model dries by wrapping them with wire or holding with clips. These (including the paper-towel-stuffing) are all removed when the paper is dry. The finished model will not only be more three-dimensional, but will be very sturdy and retain its sculpted shape.

CUTTING A SQUARE FROM A RECTANGLE

METHOD #1

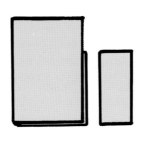

Cut along the raw edge then unfold the diagonal fold.

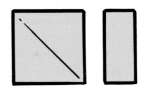

The leftover rectangular strip can be used for making smaller squares.

METHOD #2

(For a square without a diagonal crease.)

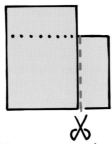

Position two rectangular sheets of identical size as shown. Cut the bottom sheet along the raw edge of the top sheet.

The undersheet is now square. If you need a second square, turn both layers over and cut the larger sheet using the raw edge of the square as your guide.

CUTTING A SQUARE FROM AN IRREGULARLY SHAPED PIECE OF PAPER

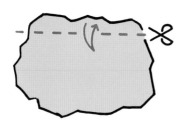 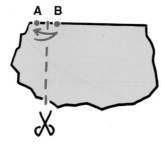  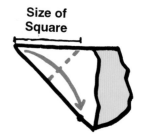

Size of Square

1 To get a straight edge: Make a fold near one end, fairly close to the edge of paper. Unfold and cut on the crease you just made.

2 Fold the straight edge on itself (point A will lie over point B). Crease and unfold. Cut on the crease you just made.

3 You now have two straight edges joined by a right angle. Fold the side straight edge up to the top edge.

4 Determine the size you would like your square to be and mark this amount at the top double raw edge. Beginning the fold at this mark, bring the point down to lie on the folded edge.

5 Cut along the raw edge and open out to find a square.

ADHESIVES

While paperfolders generally try to avoid the use of adhesives, models to be used for display (such as the Cactus Plant) or worn as jewelry may need the added security of a little glue when assembling. Here are some gluing tips to keep in mind:

- A white glue can generally be used when gluing paper to paper.
- When attaching something to foil paper or metal (such as a wire post or pin clasp), use Duco Cement ™. When using this cement on a model folded of foil paper, try not to use any on an exposed surface of the model, since it may remove the foil coating or color from the paper and spoil your model.
- Only a very small amount of adhesive is generally needed. Squeeze a little onto a scrap piece of cardboard and use a toothpick to apply.
- If possible, use a tiny clothespin or paper clip to hold the paper in place until the adhesive dries.

PROTECTING ORIGAMI MODELS

Depending on the intended use of your origami model, you may wish to add a protective coating to help preserve the model. This is especially true when using origami models as jewelry.

First experiment with a scrap of paper before coating your model, since some papers and foils may change color or become transparent from the coating medium. Check first to see if you like the new effect. Here are some methods you can try:

- **Krylon ™ clear acrylic spray.** This offers the lightest form of protection and will change the look and feel of your model the least. This spray is also useful for preventing the colors on paper you have hand-painted from bleeding if it should accidentally get wet. This spray is available in hardware, paint, or art-supply stores. Use the spray outdoors or in a well-ventilated area and spray into a box or space covered with newspaper. Paper can be sprayed either before or after it is folded.

- **Clear nail polish.** Coat your model using the brush provided in the jar. Some clear nail polishes may yellow with time.

- **Joli Glaze™.** A liquid plastic medium in a can that is sold in craft-supply stores and is a more permanent form of protection. Your model should be attached to a wire or thread so it can be dipped into the can and then hung to dry for several hours. This preservation method will give the model a glazed look; it may also cause the color to lighten, turn transparent, or bleed.

- **Sculpey Glaze ™.** This has the advantage of being water soluble. You can paint it on with a brush or thin it with water in a container so that the model can be dipped. It is sold in craft and art-supply stores. Because this glaze is water soluble, it may cause the colors on hand-painted papers to bleed.

Sources for Origami Materials

Origami USA offers a complete selection of origami books as well as a wide variety of packaged origami papers. All books and paper must be ordered by mail. They can also provide the addresses for origami societies all over the world. For a supplies list, send a self-addressed envelope with two first-class stamps to:

Origami USA
15 West 77th Street
New York, New York 10024-5192

STORES

Japanese bookstores and gift shops frequently carry packaged origami paper. Some Japanese food stores also carry this paper.

Some art supply stores may carry washi paper, marbleized paper, or packaged origami paper.

The following is a list of stores in major U.S., Australian, English, and Canadian cities and the paper they carry.

B—Origami books
M — Marbleized paper
P — Packaged origami paper
W — Washi paper

United States
Chicago
Aiko's Art Materials Import, Inc.
3347 North Clark Street
Chicago, IL 60657
(312) 404-5600
B, M, P, W

Denver
Kobun-Sha
1255 19th Street
Denver, CO 80202
(303) 295-1845
B, P

Los Angeles
Kinokuniya Bookstore
123 Onizuka Street, Suite 205
Los Angeles, CA 90012
(213) 687-4480
B, P

New York City Area
New York Central Art Supply
62 Third Avenue
New York, NY 10003
(212) 473-7705 (800) 950-6111
M, P, W

Kate's Paperie
561 Broadway
New York, NY 10012
(212) 941-9816
M, P, W

Kinokuniya Bookstore
10 West 49th Street
New York, NY 10020
(212) 765-1461
B, P, W

Yaohan Plaza
595 River Road
Edgewater, NJ 07020
(201) 941-7580
Yaohan Food Store — P
Kinokuniya Bookstore — B

Orlando (EPCOT)
Mitsukoshi
Japan Pavilion/EPCOT
P.O. Box 1000
Lake Buena Vista, FL 32830
(407) 827-8513
B,P

San Francisco
Kinokuniya Bookstore
1581 Webster Street
San Francisco, CA 94115
(415) 567-7625
B, P

The Paper Tree
1743 Buchanan Mall
San Francisco, CA 94115
(415) 921-7100
B, P, W

Seattle
Uwajimaya
6th South & South King
Seattle, WA 98104
(206) 624-6248
B, P

Australia
Japan Mart
568 Malvern Road
Prahran, Victoria
Australia
510-9344
P

McGill Authorized Newsagency
187 Elizabeth Street
Melbourne, Victoria
Australia
602-5566
P

Canada
Toronto
The Japanese Paper Place
887 Queen Street West
Toronto, Ontario M6J 1G5
Canada
(416) 369-0089
B, M, P, W

Vancouver
Paper-Ya on Granville Island
1066 Johnson Street #9 & 10
Vancouver, B.C. V6H 3S2
(604) 684-2531
P, B, M, W

England
Japan Centre Bookshop
212 Piccadilly
London W1V 9LD
071 439 8035
B, P

ORIGAMI SOCIETIES

Most origami societies sell origami books and paper, hold classes and conventions, and publish a magazine of diagrams and origami-related articles. They welcome folding enthusiasts of any age or level, from beginner to experienced. Here is a listing of some of the larger national groups. Contact the USA group for information about other countries.

Argentina
Origamistas Argentinos
Gorostiaga 1588
1426 Buenos Aires
Argentina

Australia
Australian Origami Society
2/5 Broome Street
Highgate
Perth 6000
Australia

Belgium
Vlaams Nederlandse Origami Stichting
VNOS Belgie
Post Bus 62, B2370
Arendonk
Belgium

Brazil
Grupo de Estudos de Origami
Rua Vergueiro 727, 1 Andar
01504-001 São Paulo
Brazil

Denmark
Dansk Origami Center
Ewaldsgade 4, KLD
2200 Copenhagen-N
Denmark

England
2A The Chestnuts
Countesthorpe
Leicester LE8 5TL
England

France
Mouvement Francais des Plieurs de Papier
56 rue Coriolis
75012 Paris
France

Germany
Origami Deutschland e.V.
Postfach 1630
8050 Freising
Germany

Origami Munchen
Postfach 22 13 24
Munchen D80503
Germany

Holland
Origami Societeit Nederland
Mossinkserf 33
7451 XD Holten
The Netherlands

Hungary
Hungarigami
Kecskemet pf. 60
H-6001
Hungary

Israel
Israel Origami Art Society
Mevo HaAsara 1/22
Jerusalem 97876
Israel

Italy
Centro Diffusione Origami
Casella Postale 42
21040 Caronno Varesino
Italy

Japan
Nippon Origami Association
1-096 Domir Gobancho
12 Gobancho, Chiyodaku
Tokyo 102
Japan

Russia
St. Petersburg Origami Center
P.O. Box 377
St. Petersburg 193318
Russia

Spain
Asociación Española de Papiroflexia
María Guilhou, 2-3-C
28016 Madrid
Spain

USA
Origami USA
15 West 77th Street
New York, New York
10024-5192
USA

INDEX

◆

A

Accessories, 85–107
Action models
   flying pterodactyl, 70
   kaleidoscope flower, 42–44,
      44
   kissing penguins, *77,* 77–78
   magic star, 39–40, *41*
   Jack-in-the-box, *45,* 45–47
Adhesives, 114
Animals
   flying pterodactyl, 70
   howling dog, *75,* 75–76
   koala, 71–74, *72*
The Art of Origami, 9

B

Barrettes, 104, *105*
Bases, 19–25
   bird, 25
   diamond, 19
   preliminary, 20–21
   umbrella, 23–24
   waterbomb, 22
Bird(s)
   crane, *6,* 10, 65, *66–67*
      chain of, 10, *11,* 67–68, *82*
   kissing penguins, *77,* 77–78
   sparrow, 69–70, *70*

Bird base, 25
   for chain of cranes, 67
   for crane, 66
   for kissing penguins, 78
Blintz fold, 16
Book fold, 16
Bowl, 51–52, *52*
Box(es), *48,* 48–64, *58*
   deep, 60
   hexahedron, 100
   Jack-in-the, *45,* 45–47
   masu, 56–57
   rectangular, 61
   shallow, 60
   variations, 60–61
Box cover, 57
Box divider, 59
Buttonhole flower, 82, *82*
Buttonhole leaf and stem, 83

C

Cactus plant, 84, *84*
   flowerpot for, 49–50, *84*
Candy cups, 104
Card case, 62, *63*
   variations, 64
Card holder, 64
Chinese lucky star, 92
Containers, *48,* 48–64, *58*
   variations, 60–61

Copier-designed paper, 112
Corsage, *27,* 106–107, *107*
Crane, *6,* 10, 65, 66–67
   chain of, 10, *11,* 67–68, *68,*
      102
Cupboard fold, 16

D

Decorations, 85–107
Diamond base, 19
   for howling dog, 76
   for leaf and stem
      buttonhole, 83
      standing, 81
Diamond ring, *87,* 89
Diaper fold, 16
Dog, howling, *75,* 75–76
Duo paper, 112

E

Earrings, 104, *105*
   from hexahedron, *99,* 100
   from teardrop ornament,
      90–91

F

Five-diamond decoration, 93–94,
   94, 109
Flower(s)
   buttonhole, 82, *82*
   buttonhole leaf and stem, 83
   cactus plant, 84, *84*
   corsage, *27,* 106–107, *107*
   kaleidoscope, 42–44, *44*
   standing leaf and stem, 81
   tulip, *7,* 79–80, *80*
Flowerpot, *7,* 49–50, *50, 80*
Fluted diamond, *6,* 101, *102*
Flying pterodactyl, 70
Foil paper, 110
Folds
   basic, 16
   blintz, 16
   book, 16
   cupboard, 16
   diaper, 16
   hints for, 18
   house roof, 16
   ice cream cone, 16
   inside reverse, 17
   outside reverse, 17
   wet, 112–113
Fortune cookie, from hexahedron, 100
Friends of the Origami Center of
   America. *See* Origami USA
Froebel, Friedrich, 9